THE POCKET IDIOT'S GUIDE TO

Buddhism

by Bradley K. Hawkins,
adapted by Nancy D. Lewis

ALPHA

A member of Penguin Group (USA) Inc.

Contents

Introduction

This is perhaps the appropriate place to comment on what you, as the reader, hold in your hands. It is a key to the treasures of one of the oldest and most fascinating religions of humanity. As such, it is aimed at providing the novice reader with a brief overview of philosophy, history, and (most important) the "feel" of Buddhism. But it is only the first of many keys to a vast treasury.

Because, as you are about to find out, Buddhism has changed and developed considerably over the 2,500 years of its existence, the treatment of each individual topic must necessarily be brief. Fortunately, the reader who wants to delve more deeply into the ocean of Buddhism will find no lack of more detailed studies on almost any conceivable topic of interest.

The Buddhists have a saying to the effect that after people have had the moon pointed out to them, the help of a pointing finger is no longer required. It is our hope that this small offering will be like that pointing finger, useful for your discovery of one of the noblest products of the human spirit.

Extras

The sidebars in this book offer extra information and help to explain the topics and terms throughout the book. Use these as road signs on the journey to understanding Buddhism.

On the Right Path

These boxes provide guidance about Buddhism, which supplement the materials in the text. They take a topic one step further toward understanding the religion.

Enlighten Me

These boxes will be filled with tips about the text to supplement information on the topic at hand.

What's It All Mean?

These boxes define terms familiar to Buddhism that are used in the text. Understanding the typical vocabulary and jargon of the religion helps you better understand the general subject when you encounter these terms in another context.

Bet You Didn't Know

These boxes are extra tidbits of background information that are informative or just plain interesting.

Trademarks

All terms mentioned in this book that are known to be or are suspected of being trademarks or service marks have been appropriately capitalized. Alpha Books and Penguin Group (USA) Inc. cannot attest to the accuracy of this information. Use of a term in this book should not be regarded as affecting the validity of any trademark or service mark.

Chapter 1

The Roots of Buddhism

In This Chapter

- India's role in Buddhism
- The importance of the *Vedas*
- The Sramana movement
- The Jains and nonviolence

To understand the roots of Buddhism and how the various Buddhist practices and beliefs came into being, you must first understand the historical development of Buddhism. In this chapter, we'll look at the schools of thought that influenced the development of this ancient religion that is still valuable to many people today.

Where It All Began

Most religions originated in a particular place at a particular time, and the ideas of that environment influenced the beginnings of the religion itself. Therefore, when looking at the roots of Buddhism, it is necessary to look at India and the development of other religions there.

India is a large country isolated from the rest of Asia by oceans and high mountains. These features also contribute to India's monsoon climate, which has three distinct seasons: the hot season, the cool season, and the rainy season. During the rainy season, which lasts roughly from May to October, heavy rainfall severely limits travel through the countryside; therefore, new customs and religions are slow to arrive, spread, and even depart.

India is also crisscrossed by mountain ranges and rivers that divide it into distinct areas. At around 500 B.C.E. (the time of the Buddha; see later in the chapter for more on him) the most important of these areas was the valley of the Ganges River, which flows from west to east across most of Northern India. It was here that the great religions of India first arose and flourished. Only later did they spread to the south.

 On the Right Path

> The actual dates of the Buddha and of the early events that shaped Buddhism are still matters of serious debate among scholars today. The dates given in the following chapters are those the majority of scholars agree on. But even these dates are approximate (approximate dates are preceded by "c.").

In the time of the Buddha, the Ganges River Valley was undergoing a period of vigorous religious development. Of the various intellectual currents flowing there, three schools of thought, or Indic religions, influenced the development of Buddhism:

- The Vedic religion
- The Sramanic movement
- Jainism

The Vedic Religion

The first and oldest of the philosophies that led to Buddhism was the ancient Vedic religion. The *Vedas* were the sacred books that this religion, practiced by the Aryan people, was based on. Most scholars believe the Aryan people came to India from the plains of southern Russia sometime between c. 2000 and 1500 B.C.E.

The earliest Aryans spoke a language that was the remote ancestor of other present-day European languages, including English, of course. That language developed in India into *Sanskrit*, the sacred language of Hinduism. Today Sanskrit, much like Latin, is not spoken, but read by priests in its ancient written form.

Bet You Didn't Know

Three priests would use the *Vedas* during religious ceremonies. The *Rig* was used for the reciting, the *Sama* was used for the singing, and the *Yajur* was used for the ritual performance.

What's It All Mean?

> **Sanskrit** is to the Dravidian languages what Latin is to the Romance languages—both are also dead. The relationship between Sanskrit and other European languages is close and can be seen in the comparison of key words. For instance English "brother" is "phrater" in Greek and "bhratar" in Sanskrit. **Veda** is a Sanskrit word that means "knowledge" or "wisdom."

The *Vedas* consisted of the *Rig Veda*, *Sama Veda*, and *Yajur Veda*. The oldest, and most important, religious document from the time of the Aryans is the *Rig Veda*. Made up of hymns that included blessings, praises, curses, and sacrifices, the *Rig Veda* became the main way the Aryan people praised their gods.

Cattle and Castes

When the seminomadic, cattle-herding Aryan tribes arrived in India, they dominated the agricultural people who were already living there. They created a social division known as the caste system, which consisted of the following, from the highest caste to the lowest:

- Priests (Brahmins) and scholars
- Warriors and nobles (Kshatriyas)

- Common people (farmers and merchants) (Vaisyas)
- Slaves and serfs (Sudras)

Each caste group had a particular duty to perform in society; and, in later times, when the system became more rigid, a person of one caste could not marry or even eat with individuals from the other castes. Religion was the particular province of the priestly class, the Brahmins, the highest of the castes.

Bet You Didn't Know

A fifth class is also thought to be part of the Aryan caste system and is known as the "Untouchables." These individuals had jobs in which they handled unclean objects; such lowly tasks could only be assigned to people of non-Aryan origins.

The *Rig Veda* shows us that their religion was not static. Rather, it was a living entity that changed and developed over time. Even the Indian society was shaped by the religion that came from the *Vedas*.

Out with Sacrifice, in with Brahmanism

Initially, the Aryans seem to have practiced a very straightforward religion in which the key element was sacrifice. The gods, such as Indra (the warrior king of the gods) and Agni (the god of fire), were believed to be the personification of nature's power. The Aryans believed that the gods were motivated by more or less the same things that motivated humans. Sacrifices were, thus, seen as a kind of commercial transaction in which the person who was offering the sacrifice was "trading" something to the god. In return, the sacrificer hoped to receive some favor, usually of a worldly nature, such as long life, many sons, or success in war.

Performing the sacrifice was the job of the priestly class. In the earliest portions of the *Rig Veda*, written between c. 1500 and c. 1000 B.C.E., these sacrifices seem to have been relatively simple affairs. A cow or some other animal was slaughtered, and the god was invited to come down from the heavens and join the worshippers in the feast.

Enlighten Me

The *Rig Veda* and Vedic literature aided in the development of the caste system. For example, the god Purusha was described as having sacrificed himself *to* himself. When divided, each part of his body became a different part of society. Purusha's mouth became the priests, his arms became the warriors, his thighs became the working class, and his feet became the slaves. This was all in keeping with the notion that although each part of the caste system had its role in society, it was still part of a greater whole (one body).

As time went on, the sacrificial rites became more and more complex. By the time of the Buddha in c. 500 B.C.E., some of these rituals could extend over as long as a year and require a staggering outlay of wealth and the employment of a large number of priests.

The offering of larger and more elaborate sacrifices had two effects on the development of *Brahmanism*. First, it meant that the poorer and less powerful members of Aryan society were excluded from many of the more elaborate rituals of their religion. They simply could not afford to perform the complex and expensive rituals. Moreover, the conquered peoples of the land were also excluded from the sacrifices. In effect, they were completely cut off from the religion of their conquerors. Second, it allowed the Brahmin priests to wield more and more power within Aryan society.

 What's It All Mean?

> **Brahmanism** is the term used for the later phase of the Vedic religion. This is also known as the first phase of Hinduism, which was characterized by elaborate sacrificial rituals presided over by the Brahmins (priests).

In the Brahmanic texts written between c. 1200 and 900 B.C.E., the focus of attention is not on stories about and hymns to the gods. Rather, the major theme is the correct performance of the sacrifices. Because sacrifices had become so complicated, these texts were meant to give clear instructions on how to perform them correctly.

Mixed in with these instructions, however, you can begin to see the start of a long Indian tradition of religious and philosophical speculation. These speculations centered on the creation of the world, the nature of reality, and more pragmatic questions such as the role of the sacrifices in maintaining cosmic order.

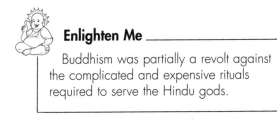

Enlighten Me

Buddhism was partially a revolt against the complicated and expensive rituals required to serve the Hindu gods.

The Sramana Movement

As time went on, the priests of the time became more convinced that their actions were not only pleasing to the gods, but that they actually compelled the gods to grant their desired results. As you might expect, the Brahmins (priests) now saw themselves as the preeminent members of Aryan society. They believed the rituals that they alone were able to perform actually generated the forces that sustained and moved the cosmos.

Meanwhile, other groups in Aryan society were considering the same basic religious questions as the Brahmins. Their conclusions were radically different from those of the priestly class, however.

These other thinkers, who seemed to have lived between c. 900 and 600 B.C.E., were known collectively as the *Sramanas*.

Not Superman, but Atman and Brahman

Instead of viewing sacrifice as concrete ritual action, the Sramanas believed that sacrifice was a "symbolic and figurative representation" of internal transformation. Thus, each element of a sacrifice corresponded to some internal action or attitude on the part of the individual. Initially, this Sramanic philosophy focused on the basic elements in life.

What's It All Mean?

> **Atman** is the Hindu idea that a pure and constant immortal soul exists that is, in some sense, associated with Brahman. **Brahman,** in Hinduism, is the underlying motivating principle of the universe: ultimate reality.

For example, the motivating principle that sustained life, *prana*, was associated with breath and, by extension, the wind. But Sramana thinking quickly went beyond these basic concerns and made even greater contributions to the religious thought in India.

Two of their most important beliefs were in the concepts of *atman* and *Brahman*. The atman was the pure spirit, unchanging and immortal. In turn, atman was a fragment of Brahman, the spiritual force that created and sustained the universe.

Because atman was immortal, the Sramanic philosophers wondered what happened to it at death when the physical body ceased to exist. The early Aryans had believed in a sort of heaven, but the Sramanas rejected this idea in favor of the concept of reincarnation.

On the Right Path

> Don't get confused by all the *Brahmins* and *Brahmans*. Brahmins (with an "i") were the priests, Brahmanism is the term for the later period of the Vedic religion (also called the Brahmanic period), and Brahman (with an "a"), in Hinduism, is the underlying motivating principle of the universe (ultimate reality).

Breaking the Cycle: Reincarnation and Karma

Reincarnation soon came to be an accepted idea in all Indic religions. But at the same time, it raised other philosophical problems. These problems became even greater when a shift occurred in Sramanic thinking sometime approximately between c. 800 and 600 B.C.E.

Before this period, the Aryan people held a generally positive attitude toward life and the created world. Life was seen as being essentially good. After this period, the Indic worldview became distinctly pessimistic—perhaps due to years of bad weather, famine, or other types of disasters. Life's pleasures were viewed as fleeting and ultimately unsatisfying.

When this new view of life became widely adopted, the process of reincarnation came to be considered a burden and something to be avoided.

 What's It All Mean? _____

> The idea of **reincarnation** is common to all Indic religions. It is the belief that human beings are "recycled" for lifetime after lifetime. Far from being a good thing, reincarnation is seen as something to be escaped from at all costs.

Another idea that developed at this time was the concept of *karma*. This concept hinged on the simple premise that all actions had reactions. Good actions had good reactions, and bad actions had bad reactions. But what about those individuals who performed good acts but suffered nevertheless? Or those who were exceptionally evil but prospered anyway?

 What's It All Mean? _____

> **Karma** is the idea that actions have effects that are inescapable, even if they do not bear fruit in the present lifetime.

Again, reincarnation provided answers to these questions. If the effect of one's actions were not felt in this life, they would be felt in the next life or even the life after that. This allowed the Indic religions to sidestep the problem of "evil." When seen from the perspective of karma and reincarnation, bad things happened to good people because they most likely had done something bad in a previous life. Moreover, those who acted improperly would suffer from their actions, if not in this life, then at a later time.

Ideas of Individual Asceticism

These new philosophical concepts shaped the ideas and goals of the Sramanic religious practitioners who tended, by and large, to be from the non-Brahmin classes (meaning, they weren't the priests) of Indian society.

If human beings were constantly reborn into a harsh world filled with suffering, then the most desirable goal available to human beings was to achieve *moksha*, which is deliverance from the constant cycle of birth and death. This could be accomplished through the reunion of the individual atman (the pure spirit) with the Brahman (the spiritual force that sustained the universe).

What's It All Mean? _____

> **Moksha** is the release from the continuing cycle of birth and death. Because reincarnation had come to be thought of as a punishment, moksha was the thing to shoot for.

How was the reunion of the individual atman and the universal Brahman to be achieved? This is where the Sramana views started to differ, but most agreed that the only way that the atman could be reunited with Brahman was through practices designed to weaken the body's hold on the atman. These practices, known collectively as *asceticism*, could include such things as fasting, celibacy, and going without sleep or even clothing. This asceticism generated *tapas*, which is a sort of spiritual power that could be used to break out of the endless cycle of life and reunite the atman with Brahman.

What's It All Mean?

Asceticism is when an individual practices strict self-denial in order to measure his spiritual discipline. Tapas is a sort of spiritual power that could be used to break out of the endless cycle of life and reunite the atman with Brahman.

We know from Buddhist scriptures, such as the *Digha-nikaya*, that many of these Sramanas practiced very severe asceticism, such as fasting and going without sleep. In addition, they vowed to do things such as never to sleep lying down, never to stay in a house, never to wear any clothes, to hold an arm above their head for a fixed number of years, or to stand on one leg for 10 years. Such deeds of asceticism are not merely a feature of the past in India; they still take place today.

In their speculation about religion, the Sramanas explored many avenues, as we can see from their philosophical books, the *Upanishads*. This series of philosophical writings was first developed near the end of the Vedic period (c. 800 to 400 B.C.E.). A number of ideas found in the *Upanishads* have parallels in Buddhist and Jain literature.

Meet the Jains

The third major influence of the Buddha's thinking was a group of ascetics known as the *Jains*. Unlike the Sramanas and the Brahmins, the Jains have a clearly defined founder, Mahavira (580 to 500 B.C.E.), who was believed to be the last in a line of 24 such Jain leaders. Mahavira was a member of the warrior class (some stories make him a prince).

Despite being married and having a son, Mahavira decided to abandon his pleasant life and attempt to attain moksha, or escape the cycle of reincarnation, by practicing asceticism. Through his efforts, he is said to have achieved *enlightenment* and been freed from the worldly cycle. After his enlightenment, he began to gather his followers into an organized group with a clearly defined program that would lead them to enlightenment, too. This program was centered on the key concept of *ahimsa*, or nonviolence.

The Jain understanding of ahimsa was a direct outcome of their understanding of karma. Karma for the Jains was an actual substance, a sort of sticky residue that weighted the atman down and prevented it from rising to the top of the universe, where it would escape rebirth. Karma accumulated as the result of bad actions, the most serious of which was taking the life of any living being.

What's It All Mean?

> **Enlightenment** is the goal of Buddhist practice. Other than the fact that enlightenment moves one to a totally different reality, the Buddhists have relatively little else to say about this concept. **Ahimsa,** first developed by Jainism, is the principle of nonviolence toward other living beings. Practices such as vegetarianism developed from this principle. Ahimsa is now a central idea of Buddhism.

The Jains felt that everything contained a life force and that many things, such as animals and human beings, had more than one such life force. It became essential for the Jains to minimize the damage they did to these living beings, because harming living beings was the easiest way to accumulate bad karma.

But trying to keep from accumulating bad karma was not in itself enough to guarantee escape from the cycle of birth and death. It was also necessary to "burn off" the karma that had accumulated before one came to the realization of the truth. Only then could he achieve enlightenment and be released from the circle of birth and death.

In the next chapter, you'll learn more about the Buddha and his teachings—the beginnings of Buddhism.

Bet You Didn't Know

The Jains, believers in ahimsa, were the first group in India to advocate vegetarianism rather than slaughtering animals for food. You might have also heard about how far the Jains will go out of their way to avoid harming other living beings, for example, having the ground swept before them so they don't harm any ground-crawling insects or praying before digging into the ground, hoping to avoid killing worms or anything else.

The Least You Need to Know

- Three schools of thought influenced the development of Buddhism: the Vedic religion, the Sramanic movement, and Jainism.

- The *Vedas* were the sacred books of the Aryans.

- The Vedic society developed into a caste system.

- The early Aryans believed in a sort of heaven, but the Sramanic philosophers rejected this idea in favor of the concept of reincarnation.

- Karma is based on the simple premise that all actions have reactions. If one's actions are not felt in this life, they will be felt in the next life or a succeeding one.

- The Jains's founder, Mahavira, developed a program that centered on ahimsa (nonviolence toward other living beings) to help others attain enlightenment, too.

The Buddha and His Message

In This Chapter

- Beginnings of the Buddha
- The Buddha's first major conclusion
- Following what is "right"
- What the Buddha looked like

You might think we would have considerable information about the life of Siddhartha of the clan Gautama of the Sakya kingdom, or, as he is better know to history, the Buddha or Awakened One (c. 560 to 480 B.C.E.), but, unfortunately, we do not. So in this chapter we will introduce you to the early beginnings of the Buddha as well as the conclusions he came to before and after he achieved enlightenment.

The Life of the Buddha

The earliest coherent biography of the Buddha, the *Buddhacarita*, was written by Asvaghosa around 100 C.E. Previous to this, our knowledge of the

Buddha's life can only be reconstructed from stray references in the Buddhist scriptures. Also found in the scriptures are a type of literature called the *Jatakas*.

The *Jatakas* describe the lives of the Buddha before his last incarnation and enlightenment. Although these tales provide us with little or no "hard" data about the historical Buddha, they are very important sources for understanding Buddhist ethical and metaphysical doctrines. Their influence is still felt today in many Buddhist communities.

In addition, you should recognize that the life story of the Buddha as we now have it is a stylized account. When you look at the biography of Mahavira, the other great religious leader of the period, you can see a very similar story to the Buddha's. These stories draw on a common pattern of Indian religious biography. The aim of such biography is not so much the recounting of the factual life of the individual as the presentation of that person as an embodiment of a cosmic truth.

On the Right Path

> The four most holy places associated with the Buddha are Lumbini, Nepal, where he was born; Bodh Gaya, where he attained enlightenment; Sarnath, India, where he gave his first sermon after he gained enlightenment; and Kushinagar, India, where he died.

The Buddha is believed to have been born in north-eastern India in the town of Lumbini, just inside the border of Nepal, in 500 B.C.E. His father, Suddhodana, was described as the king of this region, so the Buddha was born not into the priestly class but into the warrior/ruler class. His mother, Mahamya, was said to have conceived without human intervention, and she seems to have died seven days after the birth of her son. Following the customs of his people, shortly after his birth, a Brahmin priest was consulted so the young Siddhartha's horoscope could be cast and his future charted. The Brahmin informed his father that the young prince would become either a great king or a great religious leader.

Suddhodana, wanting his son to follow him on the throne, decided to carefully shield the boy from experiencing any of the disappointments and disillusionment of the world. Consequently, the Buddha was raised in a privileged and pampered environment and was taught the skills he would need to be a secular ruler. In due course, the Buddha married his cousin Yasodhara, and they had a son, Rahula. Despite living in the lap of luxury, however, the future Buddha came to wonder about the world beyond the palace gates.

One day, at about age 29, Siddhartha told his charioteer that he wanted to go out and see the city. This desire was immediately communicated to the king, who asked the young prince to postpone his outing for a day. During this time, Suddhodana arranged for all unpleasant reminders of human morality, such as the infirm and the elderly, to be hidden from his son's sight. He missed one old man, however.

Siddhartha, having never seen old age, asked his charioteer what was wrong with the man. His charioteer told him it was only the inevitable onset of old age. Disturbed by this, the Buddha made further trips outside the palace gates without his father's knowledge, and during these outings he witnessed sickness and death as well.

On Siddhartha's final trip into the world as a prince, he encountered a wandering holy man. When Siddhartha inquired about him, he was told that this was someone who had escaped the evils of the world. Deeply impressed, Prince Siddhartha decided to go and do likewise.

In the middle of the night, he kissed his sleeping wife, Yasodhara, and child good-bye. Saddling his favorite horse, he rode away from his life in the secular world forever. At first, he practiced a life of extraordinary austerity similar to that of Mahavira. He wandered the countryside naked in all sorts of weather, fasted continually, did not bathe, went without sleep, and in general performed the ascetic acts common to the Sramanas of the period. He also seems to have studied under two famous meditation teachers of the time, Arada Kalama and Udraka Ramaputra, whose names are familiar to scholars of other religious literature from the period. From these teachers, the Buddha learned how to enter the trance states that mark the practice of *yoga* even to this day.

What's It All Mean?

> **Yoga** is a series of practical stretches and exercises designed to allow the practitioner to achieve balance and clarity in his life. It is used in both Hinduism and Buddhism as well as by many other people today.

Conclusion Number One

One day, as the Buddha meditated on the burning sands beside the Ganges River, he came to his first major conclusion, namely that the way of severe asceticism did not work. Just then a passing village woman named Sujata, believing him to be a supernatural being, offered him food. He ate it, and this effectively ended the Buddha's period of extreme asceticism.

Now the Buddha recast his search for enlightenment within what he later termed "the middle way." By this, he meant moderation in all things: One should eat a sufficient amount to maintain one's health, but not too much. One should take enough rest, but not too much. This path of moderation was a radical departure from the religious practices of the times.

Despite this new regime, however, the Buddha still had not found his way out of *samsara*, the cycle of birth and death. Determined to do so, he sat down to mediate under a Bodhi tree at Bodh Gaya, a small village in what is now Bihar, India. He swore an oath that he would not end his meditation until he either gained enlightenment or died. When he arose on the full moon night of May in c. 525 B.C.E., he was no longer Prince Siddhartha Gautama of the Shakyas, but the Buddha, He Who Has Awakened.

After spending many days in meditation, the Buddha was moved by compassion for suffering humanity. Although he could now enter *nirvana*, he decided to remain in the world in order to communicate his insight to others. Over the next 45 years, the scriptures tell us, the Buddha preached his new message of salvation and gathered a large following of disciples.

 What's It All Mean?

> **Nirvana** is the goal of Buddhist practice. This is the opposite of samsara, the world that we inhabit at present. Other than its being different in every way from anything experienced in this world, the Buddhists are hesitant to try to describe nirvana.

The Buddha organized these disciples into the Buddhist monastic order called the Sangha, possibly based on the model of the Jains. He developed a complex code of rules, called the *Vinaya*, by which members of the Sangha lived their lives. He also explained his teachings in a series of talks to his disciples. These talks are collectively called the *Sutras*.

The *Vinaya* and the *Sutras*, along with a third group of texts, the *Abhidharma*, or philosophical texts, make up the sacred scripture of early Buddhism, known collectively as the *Tripitika*. The core of the *Sutras* and the *Vinaya* comes from the time of the Buddha. Later additions to these scriptures, and the development of the *Abhidharma* literature, represent attempts to clarify certain passages and to work out the implications of the early scriptures to their fullest extent.

In the early years of Buddhism, these texts were memorized by monks and passed on to their students from one generation to another. It was not until some 400 years after the death of the Buddha that they were first written down. The oldest copies of the scriptures we have today were written in Pali, a spoken language of Central India at or just after the time of the Buddha.

Written in the language of the common people, these texts were much more accessible than the scriptures of the Brahmins, which were written in Sanskrit, an older Aryan language most people no longer spoke or understood. This use of the vernacular language was, no doubt, one factor in the rapid spread of Buddhism throughout North India before the Buddha's death at the age of 80 in c. 480 B.C.E.

This emphasis on communicating the core ideas of Buddhism in everyday language is still an important characteristic of Buddhism. When Buddhism began to spread across Asia, one of the first things the missionary monks did was to translate the scriptures into the language of the people they found themselves among.

Bet You Didn't Know

The Buddha's favorite disciple seems to have been Sariputra. Sariputra traveled around India and was said to have accounted for many of the converts to the new religion. The obvious successor to the Buddha, he is said to have died a few months before his teacher. Today he is venerated as the personification of wisdom.

The monk who is responsible for the continuance of the Buddhist order after the Buddha's death is Mahakasyapa. Renowned for his asceticism and moral strictness, Mahakasyapa is said to have convened the First Buddhist Council (c. 480 B.C.E.), where the key texts of Buddhism were agreed upon and the future direction of Buddhism set. Mahakasyapa is also held to be the founder of Zen by Chinese and Japanese Buddhists. His statue is usually found to the right of the image of the Buddha in Zen monasteries.

To the left of the Buddha image is the statue of the second leader of the Zen school, Ananda. He is greatly respected as the Buddha's personal attendant. When the Buddha died, Ananda was the only monk able to recite all the Buddha's discourses verbatim.

The Three Marks of Existence

The Buddha based his analysis of the human condition on three basic perceptions he termed the Three Marks of Existence. The first of these marks or characteristics of the nature of human existence, and the foundation of the entire Buddhist religious system, is impermanence (*anitya*). Everything, said the Buddha, is in a state of flux. Nothing in the material world is permanent. Things may give the impression of being permanent, but that is only an illusion. Given enough time, everything—mountains, seas, the heavens, and especially human beings—will change and eventually cease to be. They are impermanent.

The second mark of existence, unsatisfactoriness (*duhkha*, literally meaning "suffering") arose from impermanence. All things that were not permanent were, in the Buddha's way of thinking, unsatisfactory. To place one's trust in any material thing was pointless and doomed to failure.

The third mark of existence also derived from the first. This was the idea of *anatman*. Human beings, said the Buddha, did not have a permanent soul (*atman*). For the Buddha, the human being was a composite made up of an ever-shifting cloud of physical and mental components. Thus, to talk about an eternal "kernel" of the human being that persisted after death was, in the Buddha's opinion, utterly false. Certain traits and characteristics might persist from one life to another, but not the personality per se. Moreover, all seemingly concrete phenomena in the world were really the results of constantly shifting factors. This idea, called *pratitya-samutpada* by the Buddhists, meant that almost nothing had any existence in itself independent of previous causes.

 What's It All Mean?

> **Anatman** is the Buddhist belief that no immortal soul exists, but rather a "cloud" of sensations and processes that human beings mistake for a permanent soul. Atman, as you learned in Chapter 1, is the Hindu idea of a pure and immortal soul that is, in some sense, associated with Brahman, the underlying motivating principle of the universe: ultimate reality. **Pratitya-samutpada** is the Buddhist concept that the world is not solid, but rather made up of an endless series of interlocking events.

The Four Noble Truths

But the Buddha went on from this somewhat pessimistic understanding of the human condition to suggest that one could find a way out of the human predicament. This way is the Four Noble (that is, Great) Truths:

1. Life is, in its essence, unsatisfactory.

2. The unsatisfactory nature of life stems from the constant cravings (literally "thirst") that arise in the human being and from ignorance (*avidya*) of the true nature of reality.

3. This need not be the fate of all human beings. A way exists to cease being enslaved to this unsatisfactory world.

4. The way to cessation of bondage to the world lies in the Eightfold Path.

The Eightfold Path

The eight components of the Buddha's Eightfold Path of liberation are as follows:

1. Right (that is, correct or proper) viewpoint

2. Right intention

3. Right speech

4. Right action

5. Right livelihood

6. Right effort

7. Right mindfulness

8. Right concentration

Here, encapsulated in a very few easy-to-remember steps, lies the entire Buddhist plan for salvation.

When examined more closely, this list divides into three separate parts. The first part, right viewpoint and right intention, relates to the underlying core of one's understanding of the nature of reality. In order for his program of liberation to be effective, the Buddha knew that its practitioners had to fundamentally change the way they perceived the world. This was the purpose of the right viewpoint and orientation away from the understanding of the world as made up of material things that were acted upon, and toward an understanding of the world as a series of constantly changing and interacting processes.

From this new understanding of the world came the second step on the Eightfold Path—right intention. This was achieved when the individual decided that the Buddhist analysis of existence was correct and he or she determined to follow the Buddhist plan for salvation. This meant acting in a benevolent, nonharmful manner and practicing the steps of the Eightfold Path.

The next three steps in the Eightfold Path were designed to take the insights gained from the first two steps and put them into practice in the world. Right speech, as its name implies, was based on a proper use of speech, but it really involved the entire way in which human beings interact with one another. Thus, one was encouraged not to lie, not to slander, and not to say or presumably even think anything that would upset or cause pain to another.

Enlighten Me

A carved wheel with eight spokes is a simple symbol that contains the entire teaching of the Buddha. The eight spokes symbolize the Eightfold Path, which the Buddha advocated as the way to achieve release from the pains of the everyday world. The central hub of the wheel represents nirvana, the goal toward which all Buddhists strive. Nirvana is something that is so different from the world we experience that it cannot be described. But in the truest sense, it is eternal peace.

This intention of not harming another was also played out in the next step of the Path—right action. Here, one chose not to steal, not to kill, not to use sex improperly (a rule that had different applications depending on whether one was a monk or not), not to use intoxicating substances, and generally not to do anything that would harm or upset another.

The fifth step, right livelihood, was closely allied to the fourth in that it forbade making one's living by any means that would cause harm, or being an arms dealer, selling drugs, being a butcher.

The sixth step on the Eightfold Path is quite simple. It is right effort. The Buddha did not believe that the absence of wrongdoing was sufficient to lead one to ultimate success. Rather, one needed to put forth a positive effort, both in doing good and in practicing religious exercises.

It is only when we come to the last two steps of the Eightfold Path, right mindfulness and right concentration, that we encounter actions we would consider explicitly religious. Right mindfulness was a uniquely Buddhist spiritual exercise that consisted of carefully keeping track of one's own thoughts and actions. This practice was generally restricted to monks and nuns. The practitioner of right mindfulness was urged "when walking, be aware that you are walking; when sitting, be aware that you are sitting; when breathing, be aware that you are breathing." This is the first stage in the Buddhist's effort to "wake up" and forms the foundation for the last step on the Eightfold Path—right concentration or, as we would put it, right meditation.

Buddhist meditation can be broken down into two categories. The first of these is *samadhi*. Samadhi literally means "calm abiding," which is to say calming the mind. If one practices mindfulness, one of the first things one observes is that the mind is in constant movement. Our thoughts bubble up unrequested and float through the mind in a constant whirlpool of agitation. In order for one to penetrate more deeply into the true nature of reality, Buddhists believe that it is first necessary to calm this fountain of thought. This is the goal of practices designed to induce samadhi.

The second step in this process is to practice *vipasana*, or "insight" meditation. It is through the practice of this form of meditation that the final realization of the nature of reality can be made and freedom from the endless cycles of samsara gained.

The Image of the Buddha

Early Buddhist art did not contain pictures of the Buddha. Instead, the Buddha was symbolically represented through the picture of an elephant, a footprint, an umbrella, or other images. Nor were there Buddhist temples at this early period. Many art historians believe it was not until after 300 B.C.E. that Buddhist artists began to produce actual rather than symbolic depictions of the Buddha.

It was at this time that Indian artists came in contact with Greek artists from the West. These artists were accustomed to producing lifelike artistic representations not only of everyday people, but of the gods as well. Because the earliest statues of the Buddha are from the northwest regions of India where the Greek and Indian worlds met, much evidence supports this idea.

Although some early portraits of the Buddha were done in a completely realistic manner, Buddhist artists soon developed their own ideas about how the Buddha should be portrayed. In a primarily illiterate society, Buddhist art formed a useful adjunct to the oral teachings of the itinerant preacher-monks. The statues and paintings of the Buddha quickly became stylized teaching tools. Each representation had to have the so-called "Thirty-Three Auspicious Features." These were physical marks that pointed to the supernatural origins and superior spiritual development of the Buddha. In addition, the

Buddha was often depicted as much larger than other figures in a work of art in order to emphasize his spiritual superiority.

As this formalized canon of Buddhist art penetrated throughout the Buddhist world, the effect of the Buddha's teachings were far-reaching, and as Buddhism spread, new styles of portraying the Buddha developed as well. In Thailand, for example, poses of the Buddha walking, rather than sitting, were popular, and the willowy, liquid composition of these Buddha statues cannot be mistaken for any other style. In China, Korea, and Japan, the image of the Buddha evolved to fit the tastes of these cultures. It is from these styles that we get the impression of the heavy-set, well-fleshed Buddha. In Sri Lanka, a realistic style evolved that led to many temples having large *dioramas* of lifelike figures that recount various scenes from the life of the Buddha.

 What's It All Mean? _____

> A **diorama** is a miniature, lifelike sculpture displayed such that it blends in with a painting of a realistic background.

In this chapter, we've introduced you to the Buddha, whose ideas developed into Buddhism. In the next chapter, we'll look at the development and evolution of Buddhism after the Buddha's death.

The Least You Need to Know

- The first major conclusion on the Buddha's path to enlightenment was that the way of severe asceticism did not work. He began to follow "the middle way," with moderation in all things.

- On the full moon night of May in c. 525 B.C.E., Prince Siddhartha Gautama of the Shakyas achieved enlightenment. From that point, he was known as the Buddha, He Who Has Awakened.

- The Three Marks of Existence are as follows: nothing material is permanent, trusting any material thing is pointless, and humans do not have a permanent soul and anything that proves otherwise is a result of constantly shifting factors.

- The Four Noble Truths are that life is unsatisfactory, unsatisfactoriness stems from the constant thirst for the true nature of reality, one can escape this unsatisfactory world, and the way to end this repeating cycle is by following the Eightfold Path.

- The components of the Eightfold Path of liberation are right viewpoint, right intention, right speech, right actions, right livelihood, right effort, right mindfulness, and right concentration.

- The Buddha is associated with the many statues and paintings of him that have been produced over the centuries; these depictions were not always the same.

Chapter **3**

Early Historical Buddhist Development

In This Chapter

- Four Buddhist Councils
- Three concepts of Mahayana Buddhism
- The most popular Bodhisattvas

To understand the early historical development of Buddhism, you must understand the changes that took place after the death of the Buddha. In this chapter, we'll discuss those changes as well as the topics discussed at the meetings of the Buddhist Councils, which led to the three main concepts of Mahayana Buddhism—the most important of which is Bodhisattvas.

Post-Buddha Buddhism

As with most religions, the early years of Buddhism are shrouded in obscurity. One thing is certain, however: The Sangha, the Buddhist order of monks, survived the physical death, or *Parinirvana*, of the Buddha in c. 480 B.C.E. The period between the death of the Buddha and the reemergence of Buddhism into the light of history around 250 B.C.E. is somewhat unclear, however.

 What's It All Mean?

> **Parinirvana** is the indescribable ultimate when a person has attained complete detachment from all physical and emotional suffering caused by unhappiness. It is also detachment from the states of satisfaction, happiness, and nirvana (escaping the cycle of samsara, or reincarnation). Parinirvana is the final nirvana—perfect tranquility.

The First Buddhist Council

Buddhist tradition holds that a meeting, or council, was held immediately following the Buddha's death. The major concern of this First Buddhist Council was to stabilize the Buddhist scriptures by reaching an agreement as to what were the accepted scriptures as spoken by the Buddha. For a variety of reasons, no such agreement seems to have been reached, although some general consensus was established on the basic message of the Buddha. This meant that, to a certain extent, the interpretations of what was a genuine Buddhist scripture and what was not was left up to the individual Buddhist. Leaving the canon, the total collection of Buddhist scriptures, open in this way led to disagreements later in Buddhist history.

The Second Buddhist Council

The Second Buddhist Council at Vaisali, in
c. 380 B.C.E., met precisely because a dispute arose
over interpretations of the Buddhist scriptures. In
this case, the problem lay in the interpretation of the
monastic rules found in the *Vinaya*.

One group, the Mahasanghikas, was open to a relaxed
interpretation of the rules and to the belief that an
arhant (one who had achieved enlightenment in this
lifetime) could still be subject to human uncertainties
and frailties. This was considered *heresy* to their oppo-
nents, the Sthaviras, or "elders." The Sthaviras
formed the majority of the Sangha (the monastic
order) and were much more rigorous in their interpretation of the received tradition. Unable to resolve
their differences, the two groups henceforth
went their separate ways, with a *schism* forever sepa-
rating them. A century after the death of its founder,
Buddhism began to split into different groups.

On the whole, this division within the Sangha does
not seem to have had any particular effect on the
expansion of Buddhism or on its continued success
among the peoples of India, nor did later splits in
the Sangha over other interpretations of the *Vinaya*.
Eventually, some 18 schools, or *nikayas*, of Buddhism
were to be established in early Buddhist India.

By 250 B.C.E., Buddhism's popularity in India was
extremely high. One of the greatest of India's rulers,
Asoka Maurya (c. 280–200 B.C.E.) seems to have
given his support to the Buddhist Sangha. Maurya is
best known for the series of inscriptions he ordered
to be carved to promulgate a code of behavior that

was Buddhist in tone. These inscriptions were the first tangible evidence of how greatly Buddhism had come to influence Indian life and thought.

What's It All Mean?

Schism is a formal division in or a separation from religious tenets based on conflicting beliefs. **Heresy** is the deviation from a dominant theory or practice. A schism could only take place within the order of monks, because for Buddhists schism meant a disagreement on the manner in which the monastic rules were interpreted. It naturally followed that laypersons were legally incapable of being "schismatic" or "heretical" because they were, by definition, outside this legal framework. It is for this reason that we seldom see wholesale warfare between differing factions in Buddhist history, although sectarianism did have an effect when the ruling class held to one form of Buddhism and the monks to another.

The Third Buddhist Council

In 240 B.C.E., the Third Buddhist Council was convened in the Mauryan capital city of Pataliputra (the present-day city of Patna in the state of Bihar, India). Here, the assembled Buddhist monks purged the Sangha of monks who were not sincere in their religious professions and attempted, once again without success, to declare an authoritative version of the Buddhist scriptures.

The Fourth Buddhist Council

More important for the future of Buddhism, however, was the decision to expand Buddhist missionary efforts outside India proper. After the fall of the Mauryan empire, Buddhist influence began to decline in India. But this decline was by no means swift. Buddhist missionary activity continued with notable success, particularly in Sri Lanka.

Bet You Didn't Know

Sri Lanka is a lush tropical land that lies off the southeast coast of India, only a few degrees north of the equator. It is also the oldest continuously Buddhist country on earth. The marks of Buddhism can be seen everywhere in Sri Lanka. In Anuradhapura and Polonnaruwa, the ancient and now-deserted capital cities of the north, vast ruins attest to the devotion of former Sri Lankan kings to the Buddhist religion. In Polonnaruwa, huge statues of the Buddha were hewn out of rock; these silent messengers from the past still command reverence today.

Sri Lankan kings adopted Buddhism as the state religion in c. 200 B.C.E. A number of later Indian rulers were also attracted to the religion. Notable among these was Kaniska, a king belonging to a nomadic people who had invaded and settled in the Mauryan provinces in Central Asia and Northwestern India. It was Kaniska who called together the

Fourth and last Buddhist Council sometime around 100 C.E. This Council, which is not accepted as being canonical by the Theravada school of Buddhism (the modern descendants of the Sthavira party—see Chapter 5), was yet another doomed attempt to develop an authoritative canon of scripture.

The Rise of Mahayana Buddhism

It is between c. 100 B.C.E. and c. 200 C.E. that we see the development of what was to become the second great expression of Buddhism—Mahayana.

Mahayanist tendencies are seen in Buddhism from early times, notably in attempts to emphasize the primacy of the sutras (books) over the other two divisions of scripture (*Vinaya* and *Abhidharma*). The earliest indications we have for the emergence of a distinct Mahayana tradition date from c. 100 B.C.E.

Three concepts came to dominate this emerging school of thought:

- **Sunyata.** The concept that ultimately nothing has any existence in itself.
- **The Buddha's death.** It was only an illusion.
- **Bodhisattvas.** These are people who have achieved enlightenment but took a vow that they would continue to be reborn into the world until *all* beings were saved.

Nothingness and Emptiness

Sunyata means "emptiness" and is the logical development of the earlier Buddhist concept that a human being does not possess an enduring soul and that all things are conditioned by preexisting conditions (pratitya-samutpada).

The Mahayanist philosophers took this one step further. Nothing, they said, has *any* independent reality or enduring substance. Things might appear to be solid and self-existing, but with the development of the insight gained through meditation, one discovers that this is not so. This insight, in turn, leads to enlightenment.

Buddha's Death as an Illusion

The belief that the Buddha's death was only an illusion and that he remains accessible to suffering humanity became central to Mahayana thought. According to the believers in Mahayana, only the Buddha's gross material body had died. His subtle material body and "spiritual" self, dwelling on other planes of existence, were still available for consultation to a select few. For these Buddhists, the Buddha was still alive and capable of preaching new truths about the Buddhist religion.

So from the first century B.C.E. onward, a new literature, which some claimed to be the direct word of the Buddha, arose within the existing Buddhist community. This literature, while taking more notice of lay Buddhists, seems to have been written primarily by monks. Cults arose around each of these new sutras with little or no interconnection, each being peculiar to the geographical region in which it originated.

On the Right Path _____

> It is very important to understand that Mahayana Buddhism was not a single school of thought, but rather a movement that initially gained its identity by distinguishing itself from other movements within Buddhism.

Adherents to these new texts felt they were in direct contact with the Buddha, whether through the medium of the new sutras themselves or through the more direct paths of meditation and dreams. They also seem to have held (in contradiction to other segments of the Buddhist community) that these new sutras, being direct communications from the Buddha himself, were more worthy of veneration than the *stupas* that contained only the remains of the Buddha's material body.

What's It All Mean? _____

> A **stupa** is a large mound of earth or a dome-shaped building made to hold relics of the Buddha. Some are very elaborate, erected by emperors as shrines to the Buddha. They were and continue to be popular places of pilgrimages for Buddhists.

Bodhisattvas: Enlightened and Selfless

The concept that was to have the most profound effect on the development of Buddhist thought was that of the *Bodhisattva*. Bodhisattvas were people who had achieved enlightenment but took a vow that they would continue to be reborn into the world until all other beings were saved from the cycle of birth and rebirth.

Many Buddhists were dissatisfied with the ideal of the *arhant*, the self-motivating and isolated Buddhist practitioner who was solely interested in his own release. Pointing to the example of the Buddha himself, these later thinkers held that if one were truly spiritually evolved, one would be filled with compassion for all other creatures who suffered in samsara's cycle of birth and death. Such a being would postpone his or her own entrance to nirvana in order to aid suffering people.

The emphasis in Buddhism began to shift subtly from primary concentration on the individual self to concentration on all existence. Moreover, because the Bodhisattva's spiritual development exceeded that of ordinary beings, they possessed powers and abilities far beyond those of the average man. They could render spiritual and material aid to those who called upon them. It is not surprising, therefore, that great popular devotion developed toward them. The most popular Bodhisattvas, such as Avalokitesvara, Manjusri, and Maitreya, came to be venerated almost as gods and played an increasingly central role in popular devotion as Buddhism spread out of its original Indian homeland.

The Growing Role of Bodhisattvas

With the rise of Mahayana Buddhism, Bodhisattvas became increasingly popular. In time, these figures came to dominate and even eclipse the figure of the Buddha in the minds of many Buddhists. This is not a surprising development, because the Buddha was seen as a remote figure—a great teacher and worthy of respect, but not available to help his followers in the same way as the Bodhisattvas.

Because Buddhists were often in need of worldly as well as spiritual aid, the Bodhisattvas, who were capable of providing both, took center stage for many Buddhists. The earliest of these Bodhisattvas is Maitreya. He is portrayed as residing in heaven, preparing to be incarnated as the world's next Buddha. Of all the Bodhisattvas, Maitreya is the only one to be venerated by both Mahayanists and Theravadins. (See Chapter 5 for more information on the Theravadins.)

Enlighten Me

Some Bodhisattvas have purely local cults. A good example of this is the Japanese cult of Jizo. Jizo is supposed to have taken a vow to save Buddhists from the tortures of hell. In that capacity, he is particularly venerated as the savior of children, and statues of this Bodhisattva are often placed on the graves of children.

Of the other Bodhisattvas venerated by the Mahayana and Vajrayana schools (refer to Tibet and the development of Vajrayana Buddhism in Chapter 5), the greatest is Avalokitesvara. He is seen as

infinitely compassionate and always ready to come
to the aid of suffering beings in the material world.
Artistic conventions concerning his depiction were
soon established. He was depicted as having a thousand eyes to see the troubles of the world and a
thousand arms to relieve them.

Avalokitesvara was not the only Bodhisattva to be
venerated by the Buddhist faithful. Another important figure was Manjusri. This Bodhisattva was seen
as being the embodiment of the supreme wisdom to
be gained through meditation, and because of this,
he is often represented in Buddhist monasteries. But
Manjusri is anything but a benign figure. Armed
with a sword to cut the bonds of delusion, Manjusri's
fierce countenance is a constant reminder of the dif-
ficulty inherent in the quest for enlightenment.

At first, those who adhered to the new Mahayanist
concepts (sunyata, the Buddha remaining accessible
after death, and Bodhisattvas) were a minority in the
Buddhist community, and their public behavior did
not differ in any significant respect from their non-
Mahayana neighbors. It was only later, possibly
when they had to compete for declining resources as
revived Hinduism began to eat away at their lay support in India, that animosity arose between the two
groups. In any case, Mahayana Buddhism was never
to dominate the Indian scene. Its real successes were
to come elsewhere as Buddhism spread to East Asia.

In Chapter 4, we'll look at Buddhism's spread to
East Asia and the new schools of thought that devel-
oped as it spread. We'll also examine the decline of
Buddhism in India as Hinduism asserted itself in
Buddhism's homeland.

Bet You Didn't Know

As Buddhism dispersed through Asia, new artistic renderings developed that adapted the images of the Bodhisattvas to new environments, sometimes with peculiar results. Avalokitesvara, for example, came to be venerated in China as Kuan-yin, but in art, Kuan-yin was portrayed as being female. This gender change became the norm throughout the Chinese-influenced cultures of East Asia.

The Least You Need to Know

- The main concerns of the Buddhist Councils were to reach an agreement as to what the accepted Buddhist scriptures were (as spoken by the Buddha), to purge insincere monks from the order, and to expand Buddhist missionary efforts outside India proper.

- Sunyata is the Mahayana concept that ultimately nothing has any existence in itself. Through meditation and insight, enlightenment can be reached.

- Mahayana Buddhists believe that the Buddha's death was an illusion, which allowed them to distinguish between his physical body and spiritual self. This, in turn, permitted the monks to preach "new truths" about their religion.

- Bodhisattvas are people who have achieved enlightenment but took a vow that they would continue to be reborn into the world until all other beings were saved as well.

Buddhism Begins to Spread

In This Chapter

- Buddhism's spread to China
- Four new schools of Buddhist philosophy
- Developments in Korea and Japan
- Tibetan and Vajrayana Buddhism
- Buddhism's decline in India

As Buddhism began to spread through East Asia and into China, new schools of thought emerged that meshed Chinese philosophy with Buddhist practice. This chapter covers the developments that flowed to Korea, Japan, Tibet, and eventually out of India altogether.

Buddhism Heads to China

Buddhism was originally brought to China by trade sometime around the beginning of the Common Era. It has generally been held that the first entry of the new religion into the already ancient civilizations of the East was through traders from Central Asia, an area that had been strongly influenced by Buddhism since the time of

Asoka (ruler of the Mauryan empire of Northern India in the third century B.C.E.). However, it seems reasonable to suppose that an equally important flow of Buddhist culture may have taken place along the sea routes to Southeast Asia and from there into Southern China about the same time. Whatever the case, Buddhism did not make a strong initial impression on the Chinese.

The Chinese were quite contented with their own native thought systems, such as *Taoism* and *Confucianism*, and were even somewhat repulsed by the emphasis Buddhism placed on renunciation and celibacy. These were concepts that ran counter to established Chinese ideals. Their attitude changed, however, when the stable political and social system of China began to disintegrate in the second century C.E.

 What's It All Mean?

> **Taoism** is a Chinese mystical philosophy that teaches conformity to the Tao through modest actions and minimalism (a simplistic life). **Confucianism** relates to the teachings of the Chinese philosopher Confucius, including love others, treat others well, follow good morals, and do not try to profit, gain, or take advantage of others.

A Buddhist missionary called An Shih-kao is credited with translating Buddhist scriptures into Chinese for the first time in 148 C.E. These translations were not of particularly high quality, because they necessitated the invention of Buddhist terms into the Chinese language, and at first Taoist terms were used to convey Buddhist ideas. This led to some intermixing of Taoist and Buddhist ideas in the Chinese mind. During these earliest days of Buddhism in China, short, practical texts and handbooks on meditation, rather than long philosophical dissertations, were the first to be translated.

A Buddhism for All Classes

With the downfall of the Han dynasty in 220 C.E., China entered a period of political disunity and social disruption that did not end until the rise of the Sui dynasty in 589 C.E. Despite the fact that Chinese dynasties still managed to maintain a foothold in North China, the fortunes of the Chinese began to decline. In 311 C.E., barbarians from the steppes of Central Asia swept into China and eradicated Chinese political control of Northern China for almost 300 years.

This change of political fortunes resulted in the emigration of officials and educated monks from the north to the south, where they finally settled in Chien-k'and, near the present city of Nanking. There they assisted in the establishment of the Eastern Chin dynasty and began to play a dominant role in the intellectual life of the area. From the melding of these intellectuals and religious leaders, Buddhism of the upper classes, or *gentry* Buddhism, developed for the first time.

What's It All Mean?

> **Gentry** Buddhism, favored by the upper classes in China, emphasized both Buddhist and Chinese learning and indulged in philosophical discussions and literary activities based on a mixture of Taoist and Buddhist ideas.

Buddhism also flourished in the newly constituted barbarian states of the North. Here, however, the religion developed along different lines. In the North, Buddhism was a state religion, constituted by and maintained for the purposes of the foreign rulers of the land. Monks in North China often played a political as well as a religious role in the state and were skilled in political and military matters.

The peasants in North China had a very different view of the usefulness of Buddhism. They took to Buddhism because becoming a monk offered a refuge from taxation and conscript labor. Moreover, Buddhism in Northern China began to develop ritually in ways that allowed for peasant participation, such as the making of offerings at temples, pilgrimages, and praying to various Bodhisattvas.

It is from these beginnings that the two separate and often distinct levels of Chinese Buddhism arose. On the one hand, a philosophical and meditative Buddhism was established for the upper classes who could afford to pursue religion in a leisurely manner. On the other, a more ritualistic Buddhism developed with an emphasis on supernatural aid and intervention that appealed to the peasants.

Buddhism's Golden Age in China

With the rise of the T'ang dynasty in the early seventh century C.E., Buddhism entered its golden age in China. The early rulers of the period patronized the religion strongly and sent Buddhist monks to India to obtain new scriptures for translation. Thus, certain significant figures in Chinese Buddhist history brought new life to Chinese Buddhism. These traveling monks included Hsuan-tsang, who traveled overland to India, and I-tsing, who left Canton onboard a Persian trading vessel.

This new flurry of translation was also accompanied by exciting new philosophical developments, many of which were uniquely Chinese in their orientation. Four of the most important of these new schools of Buddhist philosophy were as follows:

- T'ien-t'ai
- Hua-yen (Flower Garland School)
- Ch'an (Zen)
- Pure Land

Although all these schools agreed with the basic precepts of Buddhism as expounded by the Buddha, their understanding of those precepts was conditioned by Mahayana viewpoints and native Chinese philosophy.

T'ien-T'ai Develops

The T'ien-t'ai School seems to have originated about 550 C.E. It took its name from the mountain monastery founded by Hui-ssu (515–567 C.E.). This school, which had as its major text the *Lotus Sutra*, took an equal interest in meditation and doctrinal analysis. T'ien-t'ai developed an incredibly complex philosophical system aimed at integrating all the Buddhist philosophical schools into a harmonious whole. From this developed an equally elaborate system of meditation.

 On the Right Path

> The three movements in Buddhism are Mahayana, Theravada (Hinayana), and Vajrayana (also known as Esoteric or Tantric Buddhism). Theravada and Vajrayana will be covered in Chapter 5. Don't confuse these with the T'ien-t'ai, Hua-yen (Flower Garland School), Ch'an (Zen), or Pure Land Buddhism developments that came from an amalgamation of Mahayana and Chinese philosophy.

Hua-Yen (Flower Garland School) Develops

The Hua-yen or Flower Garland School (c. 650–750 C.E.) was mainly concerned with philosophical analysis. Starting with the concept of pratitya-samutpada (nothing has any existence in itself independent of previous causes), this school held that all phenomena were interdependent and interpenetrating. From this, Hua-yen thinkers developed a highly complex metaphysical system that greatly influenced the philosophical development of the schools that followed it.

Ch'an (Zen Buddhism) Develops

Ch'an or Zen Buddhism developed in a somewhat different direction from the heavily philosophical T'ien-t'ai and Hua-yen schools. The Ch'an School held that the core of Buddhism lay not in philosophy or text study, but in direct experience of ultimate reality. This was to be achieved through a rigorous program of meditation. Rather than depending on large tracts of communally owned land, as did the older and more established monastic orders (the Sangha), Ch'an monks wandered from place to place, relying on the charity of individuals and on their own labor for support.

Pure Land Buddhism Develops

Equally important was the development of Pure Land Buddhism. This school or schools, all based to some degree on the Buddhist scriptures titled the *Pure Land Sutras*, held that human effort was not sufficient to achieve salvation given the present degenerate nature of the world. It was therefore necessary to petition supernatural aid from Bodhisattvas or Buddhas who lived in other universes, the "Pure Lands."

These Pure Lands had not degenerated, as our world had because of the death of the Buddha. The Pure Land School believed the Pure Land Buddhas, in particular the Buddha Amida, were sympathetic beings who would, if the petitioner called their name with perfect faith, be reborn in the Pure Lands where the attainment of nirvana was assured.

Both the hearty individualism of Ch'an (Zen Buddhism) and the widespread appeal of Pure Land

Buddhism put these schools in a good position to survive what was to happen to Buddhism in China during the time that followed.

Enlighten Me

Buddha Amida is thought to be a previous incarnation of Siddhartha Gautama, the Buddha. Before Amida became the Buddha of Everlasting Light, he was a bodhisattva who refused to accept Buddhahood unless he could give eternal happiness to anyone who called upon him in the Pure Land.

The End of Buddhism's Golden Age in China

Despite support from the early T'ang emperors, the later rulers of this dynasty turned against Buddhism.

First, the T'ang emperors believed they were descended from Lao-Tzu, the founder of Taoism, and consequently the emperors increasingly came to support the Taoists.

Another reason for the decline of Buddhism in China was that many people who joined the Buddhist monastic orders were not motivated by sincere religious faith. Rather, they desired the numerous material benefits that such membership conferred and, still living a worldly life, brought disrepute on the very religion they had promised to uphold.

But perhaps the most important reason for the later T'ang repression of Buddhism had to do with property. Many individuals believed that if they donated their goods and land to the various Buddhist monasteries, they would be assured of a good future rebirth. Because the Buddhist orders were exempt from taxes, this donated property—and the revenues it could generate for the state—was effectively lost to the government.

No government can function with declining tax revenues. In 845 C.E., a strongly Confucian official petitioned the throne to suppress the Buddhist monasteries and purge the priesthood of unworthy monks. The government quickly moved to disband the monasteries. This was disastrous for those Buddhist schools that were primarily monastic (based in a monastery), but for Ch'an (Zen Buddhism) and Pure Land Buddhism, which were not monastically based, it made very little difference.

The peasants continued to patronize these two forms of Buddhism, but the golden age of Chinese Buddhist philosophy was over, never to come again. Buddhism in China now entered a period of slow decline.

Bet You Didn't Know

Buddhism is still practiced today in the Chinese countryside, although its practices have become more and more tinged with magic, and less and less concerned with "salvation."

Buddhism, Meet Korea and Japan

At the height of its prestige, Chinese Buddhism was in a favorable position to spread farther. T'ang China was the magnet that drew the other countries of East Asia to it. Consequently, ships carrying Japanese diplomats and ambassadors from the various courts of Korea constantly made their way to the imperial Chinese capital of Ch'ang-an. From there, they returned to their homelands laden not only with examples of Chinese art and technologies, but with new—and in some cases revolutionary—religious ideas.

Bet You Didn't Know

Don't think these cultures were untouched by Buddhism previous to the eighth century C.E., though. Significant evidence shows that Buddhism had, in one form or another, made its way to the Korean peninsula in the second or third century C.E. It was from there that it passed on to Japan in the early part of the fifth century. Although the Buddhism that would become identified with Korea and Japan was based on the new strands of Buddhism developed in T'ang China, it would later be refined in Korea and Japan.

Buddhism and Korea: Religion and Politics

At the same time, Korea and Japan were undergoing significant political changes. They were moving away from local autonomies and toward more centralized forms of government.

In Korea, the three kingdoms of Paekche, Koguryo, and Silla were locked in a battle for control of the peninsula. When Silla eventually triumphed in 668 C.E., the new central government wanted to synthesize the various Buddhist schools into a single, state-controlled church.

During this period of adjustment, Korean Buddhist philosophers created some of the most innovative philosophical speculations the religion has ever produced. Strongly supported by Silla and its successor states in Korea, Buddhism flourished until the thirteenth century. Eventually, the Korean form of Zen, known as Son, came to increasingly dominate Korean Buddhism. But other philosophies such as Neo-Confucianism began to thrive in opposition to Buddhism—and to receive state support. This, in addition to frequent foreign invasions and natural catastrophes, led to a decline in Buddhism's prestige until the present century.

Buddhism and Japan: Change Is Inevitable

Similar developments took place in Japan. Originally frowned upon by the Japanese as an unnecessary foreign import, Buddhism rapidly became an established "organ" of the Japanese state. At first, the emperor and his court were not interested in the finer points of Buddhist doctrine. Rather, they held the somewhat superstitious viewpoint that Buddhist rituals provided their land with better protection from natural disasters and evil spirits than did their own Shinto deities.

It was not until the late eighth century that the two great reformers Saicho (767–822 C.E.) and Kukai (774–835 C.E.) returned from China with fresh approaches to Buddhism. Saicho established Tendai, the Japanese form of T'ien-t'ai, and Kukia founded the ritualistic Tantric Shingon School. Buddhism finally began to be thought of as a *religion* rather than magic or just protection from bad things. It was not until some time later that common people began to be drawn to Buddhism in its Pure Land form, as taught by Honen Shonin (1133–1212 C.E.) and his disciple Shinran (1173–1262 C.E.).

By the thirteenth century, other changes had begun to take place in Japanese Buddhism as well. The reformer Nichiren (1222–1282 C.E.) had begun to preach an ultranationalist form of Buddhism, which held that Japan had become the true spiritual home of the religion.

Enlighten Me

Zen Buddhism places its emphasis on meditative exercises rather than scriptural study. Found predominantly in China, Korea, and Japan, Zen has been very influential in America and Europe in recent years. More on Zen Buddhism in Chapter 6.

Meanwhile, as Japan descended deeper and deeper into civil war, the emerging warrior classes came to espouse the austere tenets of Zen Buddhism as being best suited to the perilous and precarious lives they led. Thus, little by little, Buddhism became associated with patriotism and national pride in Japan. This was to have significant effects on the country in the twentieth century.

Tibet and the Development of Vajrayana Buddhism

The development of Vajrayana Buddhism (the third and latest division) is intimately intertwined with the development of the country of Tibet. Sometime around 600 C.E., a lineage of kings arose in Central Tibet around the city of Lhasa who were able to unite the Tibetan plateau under their rule. The first and greatest of these was Songtsen Gampo (c. 609–649 C.E.).

To cement his position of authority and improve foreign relations, Songtsen Gampo married two wives, one from Nepal to the south and one from imperial China to the north and east. Both of these wives were Buddhist. This no doubt contributed to the spread of Buddhism in Tibet. More important than this, however, was the fact that as Tibet became more unified, the kings of Lhasa found that the old religion, *Bon-po*, could not contribute to their political ambitions to the same degree that Buddhism could.

In addition, Tibet was beginning to look beyond its own borders for the first time. During Songtsen Gampo's reign, envoys were dispatched to India, where they modified the existing Sanskrit script for use in writing Tibetan (no small feat given that the Sanskrit script is phonetic and Tibetan is a tonal language akin to Chinese). No doubt enterprising Buddhist missionaries were trekking up the passes of the Himalayas from the other direction and over the eastern mountains from China.

The earliest arrival of these missionaries is shrouded in the mists of time, but legend attributes the establishment of Buddhism in Tibet to one particular holy man, Padmasambhava, who supposedly came to Tibet sometime in the seventh century C.E.

 Bet You Didn't Know

> A high, rocky, dry, and desolate region, Tibet has few natural resources to attract human inhabitants. Nor does it occupy a particularly strategic geographical position. Nevertheless, it has, from very early times, been the home of nomadic herding peoples.

Padmasambhava emerges from these early legends as a larger-than-life figure possessing awesome magical powers he had acquired through severe austerities, secret rituals, and prolonged meditation. Credited with subduing the dangerous and violent gods of the mountains, he is also said to have been responsible for the building of the Jokhang, the first Buddhist temple, in Lhasa during the reign of Songtsen Gampo.

The arrival of Buddhism is more clearly evident in the accounts of the mission of Shantarakshita. Invited to Tibet by the second of the Great Religious Kings, Trisong Detsen (c. 704–797 C.E.), this Indian Tantric master built the Samyé, the other great early temple of Buddhism in Tibet.

The Great Debate and the Dark Age

Between 792 and 794 C.E., the direction of Tibetan Buddhism was decided for all time. These years were the period of the so-called Great Debate between Kamalasila, the representative of the Indian Tantric form of Buddhism, and Ho-shang Mahayana, the Ch'an Buddhist monk from China. After these debates, the Buddhism of Tibet was modeled on Indian Buddhism, particularly in its Tantric form. It is from this period as well that the Tibetans began to invest considerable efforts in retrieving Buddhist texts from India and translating them into their own language.

Bet You Didn't Know

The Tibetans were so successful at translating the original Buddhist texts that even though many of those texts disappeared from the land of their original composition (mainly India), they are still available in Tibetan translations.

But all was not smooth sailing for the development of Tibetan Buddhism. The last of the Great Religious Kings, Ralpachen (805–838 C.E.), was a weak ruler and perished at the hands of his brother Langdarma. This new king was no friend of Buddhism and attempted to eliminate Buddhism from Tibet. Despite the fact that Langdarma was murdered by a Buddhist monk in 842 C.E. after a brief reign of only four years, Langdarma's tenure on the Tibetan throne marked the end of both the first transmission of Buddhism to Tibet and of Tibet's being ruled by secular kings. Here, a dark age descended on Tibet for 150 years.

This dark age ended sometime around 1000 C.E. This time the second transmission of Buddhism to Tibet began, not in Central Tibet but in the western part of the country. Here, the Buddhist teacher Atisha (c. 982–1054 C.E.) brought new teachings from the university at Vikramashila in India to the region before traveling on to Central Tibet. Likewise, in Eastern Tibet, Tibetans such as Grogma and Marpa (c. 1012–1096 C.E.) made the arduous trek to the Indian plains in search of inspired teachers from whom they could learn the latest trends in Buddhism. With this new influx of ideas came a renewed interest in Buddhist practice, and the major schools of Buddhism in Tibet date their foundations from this time.

Tibet's Major Schools of Buddhism

There are four major schools of Buddhism in Tibet. The oldest of these schools is the Nyingmapa or "Old Ones" School, which held that its origins predated this second foundation of Buddhism in the early eleventh century C.E. Unlike the other schools of Tibetan Buddhism, the Nyingmapas allowed their monks to marry and have families. Organized in only the loosest possible manner, the Nyingmapas were primarily individualistic in character and concentrated on local issues such as divination, agricultural rituals, and exorcisms.

The next oldest of the Tibetan schools is the Sakya School, which was founded by Konchog Gyalpo (1034–1102 C.E.). This school, named for its principal monastery at Sakya in South Central Tibet, was particularly known for its teaching system, called the Lamdre system, which skillfully interwove the study of *Tantra* and orthodox Buddhist scriptures. The Sakya School was also noted for its focus on a particular text, the *Hevajra Tantra*. This school rapidly began to influence secular as well as spiritual events, and when one of its head monks became the official teacher of the great Sino-Mongol emperor Kublai Khan, the emperor vested him with the secular rule of the entire country of Tibet, then a province of the Mongol Empire. Thus began the long tradition of Tibet's being ruled by the Buddhist monastic orders. This arrangement continued until 1951 C.E.

What's It All Mean?

Tantra is a form of religious practice common to both Buddhism and Hinduism that places major emphasis on elaborate rituals performed by the individual practitioner.

The Kagyu School traces its lineage back to Marpa and his famous pupil Milarepa (1052–1135 C.E.). Both these teachers were well known for their magical attainments, and Milarepa is recognized as the foremost poet of Tibet. The Kagyu were the first school to establish the concept of the *tulku*. A tulku is a highly developed monk, usually the founder of a particular order, who reincarnates and takes up residence in a new body time after time so he can continue his duties as head of his order. In much later times, the Kagyu order was one of the first to recognize the potential for expansion to Europe and America, and a number of famous modern monks such as Chögyam Trungpa and Chuje Akong belonged to this order.

What's It All Mean?

A **tulku** is the reborn head of a monastic order who is continually reincarnated into new bodies to continue his work. The Dalai Lama is the tulku best known in the West.

But of all the Tibetan schools, the most famous is that of the Dalai Lama, the Gelugpa or Yellow Hat School. Founded as a reform movement at the beginning of the fifteenth century C.E. by Tsongkhapa (1357–1419 C.E.), the Gelugpa School soon became the preeminent school of Buddhism in Tibet. Gendun-drup (1391–1474 C.E.), a disciple of Tsongkhapa, was the first head of the school to be called the Dalai Lama. His successors were seen as being, at the same time, his reincarnation and the reincarnation of Avalokiteshvara, the Bodhisattva of compassion. In 1642 C.E., the fifth Dalai Lama was appointed ruler of all Tibet, and so things remained until the Chinese drove the fourteenth and present Dalai Lama out of Tibet in 1959 C.E.

Hinduism vs. Buddhism in India

The Tantric Vajrayana Buddhism of Tibet represents the last major development of Buddhism in its home-land of India. Buddhism found itself more on the de-fensive as a now resurgent Hinduism began to assert itself. Before 600 C.E., the worship of the Hindu gods Shiva and Vishnu began to displace the numerous schools of Buddhism. This is first evident in the southern part of the subcontinent. Before this date, Buddhism had been a highly regarded tradition in South India, which was rightly patronized by the Kalabhra rulers of Southeast India. But by c. 800 C.E., Buddhism had been, for all intents and purposes, eliminated from this part of India.

However, Buddhism still held on in the northeast of the country, with large, flourishing monastery-universities that housed and educated hundreds of monks at a time. Travelers from China such as I-tsing and Hsuan-tsang reported that these Buddhist places of learning drew students from all over Southern and Eastern Asia. The monarchs of faraway states sent costly gifts earmarked for the maintenance of these elaborate institutions. It was here that the Tantric form of Buddhism evolved, and it was from here that it was exported to Tibet and beyond.

Buddhism Starts to Lose Ground

In many respects, the Buddhism of the monastery-universities had changed significantly from the rather austere faith expounded by the Buddha. Now a complex ritualism shared space with a highly developed and subtle philosophy and with an ever-expanding canon of scripture. Despite this, Buddhism continued, on the whole, to lose ground to its rivals in India. The reasons for this are not completely clear, but certain factors are evident.

India after 700 C.E. was politically very unstable. With the decline of the Gupta dynasty after 450 C.E. and its immediate successor states, India dissolved into a patchwork of petty warring states. Inevitably, life became more and more difficult for the common folk. Their overall standard of living declined as a result of higher taxes brought on by wars and by the damages they sustained in those wars.

This had two results. First, the amount they could afford to donate to religious causes became considerably less than had been the case in more prosperous times. But perhaps more important than that, they were now looking for immediate religious relief. No longer were they interested in long-term release from the cycle of life and death. Rather, they wanted a religion that could provide them with tangible results quickly. All this meant that peasant donations to the Buddhists began to drop off (although not disappear entirely) as the peasants switched their religious allegiances to the gods of Hinduism.

Muslim Invasion

Buddhism continued to limp along until it received the final blow—the Muslim invasions. These invaders swept out of the northwest inflamed with two goals: eliminating idol worship and lining their own pockets. The richly endowed Buddhist institutions enabled them to do both. Between 1000 and 1200 C.E., wave after wave of Muslim invaders plundered and sacked these last islands of Buddhist influence in India. Those few monks who escaped the wholesale slaughter of their brethren emigrated to more hospitable lands.

The Buddhist monuments and monasteries were converted for use by Muslims and Hindus, were destroyed, or sank into jungle-shrouded obscurity through neglect. It was not until the coming of the British some 600 years later that these ruins began to give up their secrets. It would be another 150 years before Buddhism was to reemerge as a living Indian religion.

Now that we've looked at the history and development of Buddhism, let's look at some of the different Buddhist philosophies in more detail, starting with Theravada Buddhism in the next chapter.

The Least You Need to Know

- Once Buddhist scriptures were translated into Chinese, Buddhism eventually developed into a philosophical and meditative Buddhism that appealed to the upper classes and a more ritu-alistic Buddhism with an emphasis on super-natural aid and intervention that appealed to the peasants.

- The four most important new schools of Buddhist philosophy that developed in China were T'ien-t'ai, Hua-yen (Flower Garland School), Ch'an (Zen), and Pure Land Bud-dhism.

- Buddhism began to decline in China because the T'ang emperors favored the Taoists, many who joined the monastic orders were insin-cere in their devotion to Buddhism, and the government lost revenues from property being donated to the tax-exempt monasteries.

- Korea and Japan underwent significant politi-cal changes in the eighth century C.E. and moved away from local autonomies toward more centralized forms of government, which aided in the expansion of Buddhism.

- The country of Tibet is intertwined with the development of Vajrayana Buddhism—the third and latest division—and the four major schools of Tibetan Buddhism: Nyingmapa, Sakya, Kagyu, and Galugpa (Yellow Hat).

- After 700 C.E., India dissolved into many dif-ferent warring states, making life harder on the commoners through taxation and wars. This led to a decrease in religious donations to Buddhism and an increase in "immediate religious relief," which Hindu gods provided.

Theravada Buddhism

In This Chapter

- Release from rebirth via personal effort
- Sangha and the way of discipline
- The life of a forest or village monk
- Sri Lanka's worldview of Theravada

Of the many schools of Buddhism that still exist, the one closest to the Buddha's teachings is the Theravada School. Theravada Buddhism is found only in Sri Lanka, Burma, Thailand, Laos, and Cambodia.

Personal Effort and Discipline

If you are looking for a simple phrase to sum up Theravada Buddhism's philosophy of spiritual practice, it would be "personal effort." The realization that release from rebirth comes from personal effort was central to the Buddha's revelatory experience.

No god could save you and no teacher could present you with the truth. It was only through personal effort that the nature of reality could be understood and the cycle of birth and death broken. Thus, salvation, in the broadest sense of the term, needed to be acquired through disciplining the mind and body.

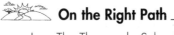 **On the Right Path** _____

> The Theravada School follows closely to the *Pali Canon*, the oldest collection of Buddhist scripture.

From the Buddha's point of view, the most important way to employ one's incarnation as a human being—itself a very rare event—was to strive for enlightenment. Because striving for enlightenment is a difficult undertaking, it came to be regarded as a full-time job for people dedicated to religion.

Rules and Regulations for Theravada Monks

The first thing the Buddha did when he began his teachings was to establish a set of rules that aspirants to enlightenment (monks) needed to follow. These rules, known collectively as the *Vinaya* or "discipline," covered all aspects of the disciple's life. The *Vinaya* still forms the framework within which the modern Buddhist monk lives his life.

These regulations lay out what food the monk can eat and when, what clothes he can wear, who he can have sex with, and many other aspects of his life, great and small. Those who follow these rules become known as bhikkhus and, in the case of women, bhikkhunis. Collectively, these followers make up the *Sangha*, the Buddhist Order who are the personification of the Buddha's teaching.

What's It All Mean? _____

> Strictly speaking, **Sangha** refers to all Buddhists. In practice, the term tends to refer only to ordained Buddhist monks and nuns, but it can also refer to an assemblage of monks and/or nuns.

It is natural, therefore, that the "professional" monks and nuns in the Sangha came to wield considerable influence in early Buddhist society. Although changes in other schools of Buddhism resulted in the Sangha being less influential, Theravada Buddhism gave the monk a prominent role in society. This was somewhat surprising, given the fact that the monks are supposed to have little actual interaction with laypeople (ordinary practitioners).

Becoming a Theravada Monk 101

In some Theravadin countries, an individual is a monk for as long as he chooses to remain in the order. In other countries, the decision to be ordained is permanent (or at least is intended to be so). In either case, the process of becoming a monk is a twofold one.

The first part of this process is called *pabbajja*, or going forth. In a reenactment of the Buddha's renunciation of his home, the aspiring monk "goes forth" from his normal home life to that of a member of the Sangha. The individual is not required to be of a certain age for this ceremony to take place. Often, parents decide to have one of their sons ordained at an early age. This is seen as having two benefits. One is to the new monk's family, who gains merit from his ordination, and the second is to the young monk himself. In times past, monkhood was often the only way to gain the education that led to high government positions. Even today, parents ordain many boys in order to receive an education.

 What's It All Mean?

> **Pabbajja** means to leave the world, begin ordination as a novice, and adopt the ascetic life.

The ordination ceremony itself is relatively simple. When it takes place is usually determined by consulting the candidate's horoscope. In addition, the young novice's new status is announced to the gods and local spirits. The candidate has his head shaved and takes a ritual bath. After this, he recites the *Three Refuges* and is presented with a set of robes and other things used by monks in their daily life. He is now an official member of the Buddhist Order, and it is from this date that his seniority in the Buddhist Order is calculated.

The new member then goes through a period of learning under the supervision of a senior monk. After several years of training, but not before his twentieth birthday, the novice may request the second step in the ordination process. This is the rite of *upasampada*. This ceremony marks the novice's full acceptance into the Sangha. After this, the monk may serve as a preceptor to younger monks. He may also serve as a member of monastic government. If a monk should choose to leave the Buddhist Order, he simply does so; no formal ceremony is conducted.

What's It All Mean?

The **Three Refuges** (also known as the "Three Gems" or "Three Jewels") consist of accepting the Buddha, dhamma (the Buddhist doctrine), and Sangha (the Buddhist Order) in a public declaration. **Upasampada** is the rite of entrance into the Buddhist monkhood; it is considered the highest ordination.

Life as a Theravada Monk

In Theravada countries, monks are generally divided informally into two groups. The first group, and the majority of modern monks, consists of the *village monks*. The village monks live on the periphery of a village and teach and serve the needs of lay Buddhists. The other group of monks, a much smaller group, is known as the *forest monks*. The forest monks continue to hold to the traditional Buddhist monastic ideal of separation from the laity, and their main activity is meditating.

Some forest monks withdraw as much as possible from contact with the world. Some cease to interact with family and friends. In addition, some cease to meet with the general public except at a few ritual events throughout the year. Thus, the monk who decides to follow this particular path must change his life radically.

These restrictions serve a clear purpose—to help the monk reach nirvana. In order to accomplish their goal, the forest monks believe that they must live disciplined lives. That discipline comes from the rules of conduct established some 2,500 years ago by the Buddha and later written down in the first of the three collections of Buddhist scripture, the *Vinaya*.

This discipline is the essential foundation of the monks' religious practice. It is only after gaining control of their bodies and minds through this life of discipline that the monks can begin to meditate effectively. However, learning to meditate is not easy. The monks must spend many hours perfecting their meditative technique.

An extensive body of literature has sprung up describing this technique. This literature discusses the eight progressive stages of knowledge (jnana), the achievement of mental peace (samatha), and finally the deep, insightful meditation (vipasyana) that leads to enlightenment and the end of rebirth.

Religious Rituals for the Laity

Unlike other religions, or other forms of Buddhism for that matter, Theravadin religious rituals for the laity are distinctly austere. Lay groups meet each lunar month on the days of the new moon and the full moon. At this meeting, which generally has a monk in attendance, the laity renew their allegiance to the Buddhist lifestyle by publicly reciting the Three Refuges and accepting the *Five Precepts* of not lying, killing, stealing, practicing inappropriate sexual acts, or taking drugs or liquor.

On the Right Path

The **Five Precepts** are not killing, not stealing, not lying, not engaging in illicit sexual acts, and not drinking intoxicating beverages or substances.

They then listen to the monk preach a sermon— usually a formal sermon rather than a spontaneous one. After this, the laity may indulge in a brief period of meditation.

Seasonal festivals have much the same character and center on events in the life of the Buddha. From one standpoint, these ceremonies do not seem to demonstrate much of a religious nature, but one must understand the strict Theravadin view on which religious functions are appropriate for different segments of society. For the Theravadin Buddhist, religious exercises such as meditation are not the province of the layperson; they are activities generally reserved for monks.

The Buddhist laypeople believe that the cultivation of this insight gained through meditation is a full-time job and one that cannot easily be accomplished in the hurly-burly of the modern world. Thus, if you want to undertake this type of training, you must dedicate yourself to it completely and renounce the world as the Buddha had done. By doing so, you earn tremendous merit and should therefore be treated with the most profound respect. In Theravada countries today, it is not unusual to see elderly women on buses get up and give their seats to teenage monks.

In a paradoxical way, the renouncing of the world gives the monk an elevated status within it. To understand this, we need to understand the essence of lay Buddhism in Theravada countries.

The Production of Merit

Laypersons can, of course, always become monks. If they choose not to, this does not mean, however, that they lack religious sentiments or that they do not participate in their tradition. Rather, they follow the path laid out for the laity—the path of merit (*punya*). In essence, the Sangha and the laity are two halves of a single entity. The monks need the laypeople to supply them with food, clothing, and the other prerequisites of life. The laity, on the other hand, need the monks as moral exemplars and a means of generating merit. But what is the point of this merit?

Here again we come back to the questions of karma and rebirth. If you know that you are going to be reborn and that a favorable rebirth depends on your good actions, it is essential to accumulate as great a stock of good actions as possible. Within

Theravadan culture, this is seen as being accomplished through *dana*, or giving. This giving is thought to be most effective when its recipients are monks. What has evolved is a symbiotic religious relationship that benefits both sides. Moreover, merit has other uses as well.

What's It All Mean?

> **Punya** is the idea that good actions produce merit. This merit can then be "traded" to the gods in return for material favors. **Dana** is the most important lay virtue; it consists of generously giving material goods away, especially to Buddhist monks.

Although Theravadins do not believe gods can lead them to ultimate freedom, they are still seen as having their uses. When a person needs help with the crops, sickness, love, and so forth, it is useless to consult the Buddha (not considered a god) and his monks, because these worldly problems are not their area of concern. The gods can help, but they need to be coerced. This is done through the transfer of merit.

Because Buddhists do not see the gods as immortal, only very long-lived, they believe the gods will be reborn just as humans will be. This being the case, the gods need merit as well if they are to be reborn in a good condition. But the nature of being a god makes it impossible, for a variety of reasons, to generate such merit. Thus, the gods are dependent on human beings in that they can acquire merit only if humans transfer it to them, which the Theravadin Buddhists are happy to do in return for worldly considerations.

Lay Buddhists and Monks Celebrate Together

The emphasis placed on meditation for monks means that they spend much of their time separate from ordinary practitioners (the laypeople). But this is not always the case. On the great Buddhist holidays, the two groups interact.

In general, Buddhist festivals are structured around events from the life of the Buddha. Moreover, because the festivals developed within the context of agricultural societies, they also tend to bear some relationship to the cycle of planting and harvest. Other festivals, such as the beginning of the New Year, vary from one society to another.

In Theravada countries, regular fortnightly days (14 days, or 2 weeks) based on the appearance of the full and new moons are set aside for religious observance. These days, called *poya days*, correspond loosely to the European or American Sunday or Sabbath days. On these days, laypeople observe the Five Precepts.

Laypeople often spend the day in religious pursuits such as going to hear a sermon delivered by a monk and practicing a small amount of meditation. This is the general pattern followed on all religious holidays, which occur on the poya days of particular months. Poya days are not celebrated in non-Theravada Buddhist countries.

 What's It All Mean? _____

> **Poya days** are considered the "Sundays" or Sabbath days of Theravada Buddhism. They happen twice each lunar month on the day of the full and new moons. On these days, pious Buddhists perform a variety of religious activities, including giving food to the monks, listening to sermons, and strictly adhering to the Five Precepts.

For the Theravada Buddhists, the most important celebration of the year is the full moon day of May, known as *Wesak*. The birth, enlightenment, and death of the Buddha are all believed to have happened on this day (albeit in different years). Another important festival falls on the full moon day of June. This marks the beginning of the three-month-long Rain Retreat (sometimes called the Buddhist Lent). During this time, the monks withdraw from society in order to practice meditation more intensively. Laypersons also attempt to adhere more strictly to Buddhist principles during this period. The Rain Retreat ends with *Kathina*, where laypersons bring the monks new robes and other necessities of life.

Some festivals are practiced only in certain areas. For example, the festival of *Poson* celebrates the bringing of Buddhist teaching to Sri Lanka in the second century B.C.E. Likewise, the observance of *Esala* takes place only in Sri Lanka. It is marked by a huge parade, called the *Esala Perihara*, in Kandy, at which time the holy tooth relic of the Buddha is displayed. In other Theravada countries, other local festivals take place as well. Although these festivals are serious events, they are also enjoyable occasions.

The Theravada Worldview in Sri Lanka

In present-day Sri Lanka, some 75 percent of the island's population still follows the precepts of the founder of Buddhism, Siddhartha Guatama, as Buddhists have done since the beginnings of the religion in c. 500 B.C.E.

Moreover, many Sri Lankans elect to pursue their religion more deeply through entrance into the Sangha—the Buddhist Order of monks and nuns. Today, no official Buddhist nuns reside in Sri Lanka, but this was not always the case. Buddhism has long been noted for its positive attitude toward women, and women have pursued enlightenment on an almost equal footing with men for much of its history.

For the Sri Lankans, Theravada Buddhism is a living faith that shapes their entire lives. Nowhere is this more evident than in Kandy, the capital of the last independent kingdom to exist in Sri Lanka before it was governed by the British in 1815.

Bet You Didn't Know

The lack of Buddhist nuns in present-day Theravada countries reflects an historical accident rather than deliberate sexism. Indeed, women still play a very effective, if unofficial, religious role in Theravada Buddhist countries. Moreover, a movement is strengthening to reintroduce the ordination of nuns in the Theravada countries. Nuns still exist in Mahayana and Vajrayana Buddhism.

Kandy: The Center of Sri Lankan Buddhism

Built in a sheltered valley deep in the central hill country, Kandy has long been considered the center of Buddhism in Sri Lanka. Wherever you look, the Kandyans' devotion to Buddhism is evident.

Near Kandy's central lake lie two of the most sacred Buddhist sites in Sri Lanka. One is the Dalada Maligawa, the Temple of the Tooth, so called because it houses a supposed relic of the Buddha—one of his teeth.

Across the lake from the Dalada Maligawa is Malvatta, the great central monastery of the Siyam Nikaya, the largest single group of Buddhist monks on the island. Not far away, at the other end of town, is the other major monastery in Kandy, Asgiri, the central monastery of the second largest group of monks.

Throughout Kandy and in the surrounding country-side, numerous tiny shrines and monastic residences attest to the devotion of the common people to their religious roots.

A Modern Theravada Buddhist Community

Not all Buddhist buildings in Sri Lanka are old. In the mountains about five or six miles south of Kandy, a new Buddhist community has developed. Built into the steep hillside, it serves as a center both for the local population and for interested foreigners who want to sample Buddhist culture.

Like all Theravada Buddhist establishments, it presents the foreigner with two seemingly contradictory pictures of Buddhism. On one hand, the shrines to the Buddha are sumptuous, colorful, and complex. On the other hand, the monks live in surroundings of the utmost simplicity. Yet these contradictory images form a seamless whole in the Theravadin worldview.

Upon entering the monastery, worshippers first see the great stone arch that marks the boundary between the regular, everyday secular world and the sacred world of the monastery. No elaborate sign marks the division, just a stone gate surmounted by a carved wheel with eight spokes representing the Eightfold Path (see Chapter 2).

Crowning the monastery at the top of the hill is the main shrine dedicated to the Buddha. On entering this shrine, worshippers are cradled by cool semi-darkness. The interior is lit only by the light from a few narrow windows high in the walls and some candles burning on the altar. Instinctively, all conversation ceases. Everything in the hall is designed to quiet the mind and draw the worshippers' attention to the central figure of the Buddha.

Enlighten Me

Buddhists believe both that life is ultimately an unsatisfactory experience and that after we die we are reborn into the world time after time. The many gorgeous shrines dedicated to the Buddha are constructed to honor the great teacher who revealed to human beings the way to escape from the pain of samsara, the cycle of death and rebirth.

This statue of Lord Buddha stands some 15 feet in height. The Buddha is represented as being this tall, not because Buddhists believe him actually to have been this height, but in order to symbolize the greatness of the Buddha's virtues. It is a riot of bright colors—oranges, blacks, reds, and greens—all used in such a manner as to create the image of a living being. All the other statues representing the Buddha's first disciples that surround the central figure are likewise painted in bright colors so they appear at first glance to be living beings frozen in time and space.

Directly in front of the Buddha figure lies the altar. Because the daily *puja* of offerings is made here, the altar table is covered with bowls of fruit, flowers, and water. This practice of making symbolic offerings rather than sacrificing animals (or even people) appears to have been originated by the Buddhists and even spread to Hinduism. Its intent is not to bribe or appease an angry deity, but to render thanks and praise to a revered teacher. On each side of the altar stand candles that form the symbolic offerings of light. The faint, sweet, smoky scent of incense is everywhere. Around the walls are still more figures that graphically depict the life and teaching of the Buddha.

Enlighten Me

Most of the time, the only ones who attend the daily puja are the monks who live at the monastery. This changes on the days of the new moon and the full moon. These holidays (poya days) are Theravadin holy days, and many villagers join the monks in their religious devotions.

Just below the shrine are the other monastery buildings. On the right is a large building that is used as a school. Here, regular classes are held to teach children the basics of the Buddhist religion. Here, too, classes are held for interested foreigners. When not being used for religious teaching, the schoolrooms are used as a regular school. This link between Buddhism and education has been present since the very beginning of the religion. Other buildings house the guests' sleeping quarters, administrative offices, and the kitchen.

Bet You Didn't Know

A kitchen is something of an innovation at a monastery. Traditionally, Theravadin Buddhist monks, with their shaven heads and distinctive orange robes, have gone out at about 9 A.M. and begged for food from house to house in nearby villages. After collecting their food, the monks would return to the monastery and eat before noon, because monastic rules forbid eating solid food any later than noon.

Nowadays, with the influx of foreign students, the monks at newer monasteries have kitchens. They do not, however, do their own cooking, which is still forbidden. Rather, women from the village vie for the honor of cooking the monks' food. For Buddhist laypeople, to give things to the monks or to perform service for them is a sure way to gain merit and a better rebirth.

Farther down the slope, away from the hustle and bustle of the main compound, are the actual living quarters of the monks. Each monk has his own hut. In his dwelling, the monk has a bed, a desk and chair, and perhaps some books. How the monk spends his day generally depends on his assigned duties.

In this chapter we've looked at one school of Buddhism, Theravada Buddhism. In the next chapter, we'll look at another school, Zen Buddhism, the way of meditation.

The Least You Need to Know

- Central to the Buddha's revelatory experience was the realization that release from rebirth came from personal effort.

- The Sangha, the Buddhist Order, is the personification of the Buddha's teaching.

- The village monks' main jobs are teaching and serving the needs of lay Buddhists. The forest monks' main activity is meditating.

- For the Theravadin Buddhist, religious exercises such as meditation are not the province of the layperson; they are activities generally reserved for monks.

- Good actions, such as the giving of material goods liberally to Buddhist monks, can produce merit, which can then be traded to the gods in return for material favors.

Zen Buddhism

In This Chapter

- Zen meditation and awakening
- Can you answer a koan?
- Mindfulness to achieve enlightenment
- The Eihei-ji monastery monks

Zen Buddhism stands in sharp contrast to Theravada Buddhism both geographically and ideologically. The original home of Zen was India, but it was not until it was carried to China, and then to Korea and Japan, that it reached its fullest potential.

The Way of Zen Meditation

Given the ever-present emphasis on meditation in Buddhism, it isn't surprising that monks in other parts of the Buddhist world developed meditative techniques appropriate to their own societies. One of the most radical of these schools is the form of Buddhism known in the West by the generic term *Zen*.

The course Zen Buddhism initially followed was different from that of most other schools of Buddhism.

These other schools tended to congregate in monasteries that, over the centuries, came to acquire more and more property. Thus, the monks found themselves in a peculiar position. Individually, they were as poor as the Buddha's original followers. Collectively, however, they were often rich beyond the dreams of ordinary materialism. Increasingly, they sank these funds into large buildings, elaborately adorned and richly furnished.

Although this impressed outsiders, a growing feeling arose among some of the monks that such frills were dangerous distractions from the essential business of gaining release from the cycle of birth and death. These new intellectual currents affected the development and orientation of Zen, and, indeed, led to the goal of living life consciously and deliberately.

A Spiritual Awakening

Philosophically, the essence of Zen is that all beings are already enlightened. They simply don't know it yet. Therefore, the goal of Zen is to awaken people to their own spiritual nature. This is accomplished not through books or intellectual activities, but through meditation. Zen meditation is designed to overcome the rational, dualistic mind and lead the practitioner to the unifying ground of existence we all share.

Two basic forms of Zen meditation exist. The first, practiced by the Soto School, consists of emptying the mind and achieving a deep meditative state. This is accomplished through techniques such as paying attention to your breathing. According to the Soto

School practitioners, if you penetrate deeply enough into this meditative state, you will come to the realization of the true nature of reality and thereby achieve enlightenment.

The second method, practiced by the Rinzai School, has the same goal. It differs from Soto, however, in its use of *koans*. A koan is a form of riddle that seems to have no logical answer. Some of these koans (such as "What is the sound of one hand clapping?" or "Does a dog have the Buddha nature?") have become famous even outside the Buddhist tradition. The point of the koan exercise is to break through dualistic, mundane logic and thus come to know the true nature of reality.

 What's It All Mean?

> A **koan** is a device, usually in the form of a short paradoxical question, used in Zen Buddhist training as a means of shocking individuals out of their dualistic thinking. This forces the practitioner to "turn off" the logical reasonable mind. Very often the questions have no real answer.

This meditative training, along with Zen's emphasis on simplicity, might lead you to think that Zen has done away with the more ritualistic side of Buddhism. Indeed, it was this assumption that first attracted many American and European converts to Zen Buddhism just after World War II. But in fact, this is not the case.

Zen Rituals

Zen was influenced by the wishes of its patrons, the wealthy and powerful ruling classes of Japan. These classes, who often saw religion and government as two sides of the same coin, were often more interested in Zen monks' perceived ability to perform powerful protective rituals than in the philosophical and meditative practices they advocated. Although this type of activity found its fullest expression in other Buddhist schools such as *Shingon*, all the Japanese Buddhist schools were, to some extent, tinged with this ritualistic emphasis.

What's It All Mean?

> **Shingon** Buddhism's teachings are known as Shingon Esoteric Buddhism. It is a religion that was established by Kôbô Daishi (Kûkai) at the beginning of the Heian period (ninth century C.E.).

Consequently, ritual had, and still has, an important place in Zen Buddhism. The goal of using rituals, like the Theravadin monks' code of discipline, is to sharpen the monk's attention so he is consciously aware of everything he does. This "paying attention" is called *mindfulness* and has always been seen in Buddhism as one of the primary ways of achieving enlightenment.

Buddhist monasteries and temples usually have a morning and an evening service presided over by either the abbot (the monastery superior) or the chief priest of the temple. Laypersons can attend these ceremonies, but except for the great Buddhist holidays, the ceremonies tend to be for religious specialists only.

What's It All Mean?

> **Mindfulness** is the foundation for all Buddhist spiritual practice. It is the idea that one must "wake up" and live life consciously and deliberately.

At these ceremonies, fruit, flowers, and incense are offered to the Buddha and the major Bodhisattvas (see Chapter 3) such as Manjusri and Avalokitesvara. Various texts are chanted, particularly the *Heart Sutra*, a brief scripture that encapsulates the philosophical teachings of Zen. Officiants often wear elaborately embroidered silk robes that seem very far removed from the austere life preached by Zen. (All this comes as something of a shock to American and European practitioners who have learned their Zen from books and not from living teachers.)

Zen Religious Celebration

As in the Theravada Buddhist countries, the Japanese Zen Buddhist monks and the laypeople come together to celebrate important religious dates. But Mahayana Buddhist (which Zen is a part of) religious holidays often vary from those of Theravada countries.

In Japan, the largest Mahayana country, the Japanese Buddhists do not celebrate the birth, enlightenment, and death of the Buddha on the same day as their Theravada cousins in Sri Lanka and Southeast Asia. The Buddha's birth (Hana Matsuri) is celebrated on April 8, his enlightenment (Nehan) is celebrated on February 15, and his death (Rohatsu) is recognized on December 8. Rohatsu marks a one-week period of intensive meditation.

Of particular importance to Japanese Buddhists is the four-day festival of Obon, which starts on July 13. This festival commemorates the release of the mother of Maudagalyayana (a disciple of the Buddha) from one of the Buddhist hells. In Japan, it has become a festival of remembrance of one's deceased ancestors.

Some festivals are strictly of importance to Zen practitioners. In October, the festival commemorating Bodhidharma (the first teacher to bring Zen from India to China) is celebrated. Great Japanese Zen teachers are honored as well. Rinzai Zenji is remembered on January 10, Daito Zenji on November 22, Dogen Zenji on August 28, and Keizan Zenji on August 15. Pure Land practitioners honor their founder, Shinran, on May 21.

The Zen Worldview in Japan

In some ways, a Zen Buddhist monastery is remarkably similar to a Theravada Buddhist monastery. It has the same sense of quiet and of serious purpose, but in many other ways, a real difference exists. Even the monks look different. Like their Theravadin cousins, they shave their heads, but instead of loose orange robes, these monks wear somber black ones more fitted to the colder climates of Northeast Asia.

A good example of both the similarities and differences between Sri Lankan and Japanese monks can be seen at the Soto Zen head monastery of Eihei-ji.

Bet You Didn't Know

> In the Soto School of Zen, the practitioner can often "just sit" (*Shikan-taza*) because this school believes that the very act of concentrated meditation is in itself sufficient to lead to enlightenment.

Eihei-ji: The Austere Simplicity of Zen

The Eihei-ji monastery was founded in 1243 by the great Japanese Zen master Dogen. Built in dense forests on the isolated mountains of Western Japan, this monastery is still noted for the rigor of its training discipline. One can see the emphasis Zen places on interior introspection in the very architecture of the monastery. Eihei-ji is surrounded by a plain wall with only one or two gates that are typically left closed and barred. But once inside those walls, a whole new world opens up.

Like most traditional Japanese monasteries, Eihei-ji is constructed around a series of courtyards. These courtyards often contain small gardens, either with plants or abstract arrangements of rocks and sand.

The rooms are separated by screens of rice paper, and the floors are covered with tatami, mats of woven rushes that give the rooms a distinctive smell. These rooms often have no furniture and are furnished only with a few cushions.

At night, the rooms double as sleeping quarters when sleeping pads called futons are taken from nearby cupboards and unrolled. The only decoration may be a small wall niche in which hangs a simple ink painting or perhaps a pithy Zen saying in fine, ink-brushed calligraphy. In front of this sits a small vase with a few carefully arranged flowers. This austere simplicity is designed to promote a calm and peaceful atmosphere conducive to meditation.

The Life of a Zen Monk

Many of the monks training in the monastery will be there for only a relatively brief period of time. Only a few monks choose to dedicate themselves to the quest for enlightenment and spend their entire lives in the monastery.

The training schedule in Eihei-ji is not for the weak. Although monks in Theravada countries tend to have their own separate living space, monks in Zen monasteries often live in dormitories. Monks are awakened before sunrise and bathe in cold water. Then they proceed to the shrine room and conduct the morning worship service.

Because the earliest writers on Zen in European languages emphasized meditation, often to the point that they ignored or downplayed other aspects of

Zen practice, many Europeans and Americans have assumed that Zen is without ritual or scripture. In fact, as is the case in other schools of Buddhism, Zen has many colorful and complex rituals designed to pay homage to the Buddha.

Enlighten Me

In Japan, it has become the custom to allow monks to marry. This is not the case in most schools of Buddhism, however. It has also become the custom for sons to inherit their fathers' positions as heads of the local Zen temples scattered throughout Japan. In order to do so, however, the sons must prove that they have attained a certain degree of proficiency in meditation. This is acquired through a two- or three-year course of training in the monastic setting.

But for the true Zen practitioner, all these actions are used to deepen their meditation. When a Zen monk goes to the bathroom, sits down to eat, or gets ready for bed, a prescribed ritual is performed. Indeed, the entire life of the Zen monk is defined by such rituals. It must be remembered that these rituals are not seen as being important in themselves. Rather, they are viewed as a means to an end.

After morning worship, the monks of Eihei-ji begin the first of several periods of meditation that last between an hour and an hour and a half. The first thing Zen meditators are taught is the proper posture for meditation, the *lotus position*.

On the Right Path

> The lotus position is more than just sitting cross-legged on the floor. The proper form of the lotus position is as follows: The buttocks are elevated by means of a cushion so that the back is straight and the head erect, and the hands are folded in the lap.

After meditation, the monks can at last have something to eat. The diet at a Zen monastery tends to be vegetarian. Unlike Theravada monks, who are allowed to eat meat if it has not been killed specifically for them, Zen monks must take in no animal protein. This is why so much emphasis is placed on eating vegetable proteins, such as bean curd, and on the proper balance of different food types. This has been popularized in Europe and America as the macrobiotic diet.

The monks are also not allowed to smoke or drink, at least while they are in training. Like all other activities, eating and cleaning up afterward are done in a deliberate, ritualistic way. After breakfast, the monks undergo more meditation until the middle of the afternoon, when another meal is taken. Then they disperse to attend to the maintenance of the monastery and their own few belongings. The day ends near sunset with another worship service. After this, the monks are allowed either to sleep or, if they wish, to meditate on their own into the night.

Now that we've looked at two schools of Buddhism, Theravada and Zen, let's look at the third, Vajrayana Buddhism, in the next chapter.

The Least You Need to Know

- The goal of Zen is to awaken people to their own spiritual nature, which is accomplished through meditation.

- Ritual has an important place in Zen Buddhism. The goal of using rituals is to sharpen the monk's attention so he is consciously aware of everything he does.

- The followers of the Soto School of Zen achieve a deep meditative state by emptying the mind; the Rinzai School uses koans (unanswerable questions) during meditation to come to know the true nature of reality.

- Few monks choose to spend their entire lives in the monastery on the quest for enlightenment; most monks are in training at the monastery for only a brief period of time.

Vajrayana Buddhism

In This Chapter

- The way of ritualism
- Tantric practice and initiation
- Differences in Tibetan Buddhism
- The Gelugpa School of Vajrayana

Sometime around 500 C.E., another set of religious developments was taking place in India. It was at this time that both Hinduism and Buddhism began to exhibit those traits of the practice we now call *Tantra*.

Tantra seems to have been an attempt to develop a new form of practice that was more dynamic than the static meditations of earlier Buddhism. In the process, a radical new form of Buddhism emerged—Vajrayana Buddhism.

The Way of Ritual Practice

Vajrayana Buddhism starts from somewhat different premises than other forms of Buddhism. This difference is not so much one of philosophy as it is of methodology. Vajrayana Buddhism, far from dismissing the body as a means of achieving enlightenment, embraces it.

Consequently, the Vajrayana Buddhist monk's training is somewhat different from that of the Theravadin or Zen monk. The following is a breakdown of the different forms of training:

- The essence of Theravada training is the perfection of meditation through monastic regulations and the knowledge of the *Pali* scriptures.
- The essence of Zen training is the perfection of meditation through self-discipline.
- The essence of Vajrayana training is the perfection of meditation through ritual practice.

On the Right Path

> Notice that Pure Land Buddhism isn't in the training comparison list. This is because the basic tenet of Pure Land Buddhism is that salvation depends on faith more than on works and meditation.

But this emphasis on ritual performance comes relatively late in the monk's career. First, he is required to undergo a long period of scriptural study to prepare for his ritual studies.

Tantric practices are seen as extremely effective in leading the practitioner to nirvana, but they are extremely dangerous as well. To approach them without intense preparation is not wise and can lead to reincarnation in one of the numerous Buddhist hells. It is for this reason that laypeople tend to avoid Tantric practice, leaving its use to religious specialists.

Understanding the Tantric Path

Initiations are a particular feature of Tibetan Buddhism. The tradition this school developed out of is Tantra. Tantra is something that cannot be done by oneself. It can be learned only at the feet of a guru who has himself traveled the path that the practitioner wants to follow and who can guide him or her by experience.

Indeed, the guru is seen as being of such great importance that he is often venerated as a deity in his own right. Many of these highly developed gurus are seen as being able to reincarnate over and over again at will. These are the *tulkus* (discussed in the "Tibet's Major Schools of Buddhism" section in Chapter 4). Under the guidance of an experienced guru, the novice enters the Tantric path.

The Preliminary Practices

The Tantric path begins with the preliminary practices. These practices may vary from school to school, but they have certain common elements.

The first of these is prostration. Here, the practitioner stretches out full length on the floor in front of a shrine to the Buddha and then rises completely to his feet again. This practice is to be performed 100,000 times over the course of his study.

He will also perform 100,000 repetitions of various ritual offerings and repetitions of formulas designed to purify and focus his mind. But remember, none of these practices are actually Tantric in themselves. These practices, which take years and beyond which many people never go, are designed to test the would-be Tantric practitioner and purify him for the work ahead.

This being said, the practices are also thought to have value in themselves, and many people, particularly laypersons, perform these rites without any thought of progressing beyond them to the actual study of Tantra, which is generally seen as the realm of monks and nuns. Such practitioners see these practices as bearing fruit in some future existence.

All the practices are regarded as necessary if the practitioner is to develop the essential base of ethical and spiritual purity needed to attempt the difficult and dangerous Vajrayana path. The higher initiations that follow these preliminary practices allow the practitioner to undertake specific forms of meditation.

Enlighten Me

Tibetan Buddhists believe that the higher the spiritual attainment of the guru, the more effective the initiation. Because the current Dalai Lama is the spiritual head of the Tibetan tradition, many people, both men and women, travel to receive his initiation. Most of the people attending the initiation do not intend to enter into serious practice and be ordained into the Sangha (Order). Rather, they believe that the initiation will bear fruit in a future life (should they then attempt serious practice) and create the conditions that will lead to enlightenment. In a sense, it is future life insurance.

The Initiation

Once the student completes his preliminary practices, he is ready to be initiated by his guru. This ritual, the *abhiseka*, is central to the student's study. Without it, even if he has access to the Tantric texts, his study would be in vain. The abhiseka not only authorizes a person's practice, but it empowers it as well. Perhaps more important, it places the student in the "family" of those who use the particular text or texts named in the ritual. This qualifies the practitioner to receive the oral teachings that have been passed down from teacher to student concerning the meaning of a particular text. In short, the abhiseka is an event of great importance.

What's It All Mean?

> The **abhiseka** (literally "sprinkling") is a ceremony held mainly in Vajrayana Buddhism to initiate the student into a higher level of study. The number of initiations varies from one tradition to another.

In modern society, we believe that texts should be self-explanatory. But in the Tantric traditions, the text is seen as far too dangerous to offer a clear meaning. The knowledge contained in the text could cause harm to others if individuals applied their own interpretations. As a result, the texts are often written in confusing and enigmatic language, sometimes called *twilight language*. This means that the texts themselves are not the primary vehicle for transmitting the teaching, but rather serve as a sort of memory aid for the teachers and students in the study of the much more important oral tradition.

 What's It All Mean?

> **Twilight language** can only be interpreted through the guidance of a guru or teacher. It is a deliberately obscure way of writing designed to protect its teachings from unauthorized practitioners.

Vajrayana Buddhists appear to believe in the vast pantheon of gods and goddesses. For the practitioner of Tantra, however, these deities are not so much actual, existing entities as what we would call archetypal symbols for psychological processes and neuroses. As such, they provide the practitioner with a way of interacting with factors in his own mind that might otherwise only exist at an unconscious level and thus be inaccessible in other ways.

At the time of initiation, the guru, who is experienced with such questions, selects a *yidam* (personal deity) for the student to work with. Likewise, he shows the student the appropriate *mantra* (meditation formula) for that deity. This mantra, usually of Sanskrit origin, encapsulates the essence of the yidam in a short phrase that the student can mediate on at all times and in all places in daily life. Through it, the student maintains a constant spiritual connection with his inner self.

The *mandala* is used in more formal religious practice. It is a complex drawing that in effect unites the universe, in all its complexities, with the student. Through the mandala, a sacred space is created that unites the two. The mandala becomes a sort of sacred road map that describes the journey of the student to the "palace" of the yidam. By ritually and meditatively following this map, and overcoming the various obstacles that confront him, the student moves closer to the ultimate goal of uniting with the yidam. Such a union is the culmination of the student's practice. Through it, he recognizes his identity with ultimate reality and thus achieves release (nirvana) from the cycle of birth and death (samara).

> ### What's It All Mean?
>
> A **yidam** is a personal deity who plays a central part in the practitioner's meditative and ritual life. A **mantra** is a sacred formula used in some forms of Buddhist meditation. Although common to all forms of Buddhism, it is particularly utilized in Tibetan practice. A **mandala** is a sacred drawing or design that provides the practitioner with a sort of "road map" of reality.

Enlightenment in One Lifetime (Tibetan Buddhism)

Tibetan Buddhists believe that because people have different talents and abilities, each individual must use a different combination of techniques to leave the cycle of birth and death. As in all other Buddhist schools, meditation is seen as a major tool in this quest, but Tibetan Buddhists also believe that enlightenment can be achieved through the power of ritual. This dual approach sets Tibetan Buddhism apart from other Buddhist schools which feel that ritual is always subordinate to meditation and that progress toward enlightenment is gradual over a series of lifetimes.

The Tibetan School believes that an individual can achieve enlightenment in one lifetime. The suddenness of enlightenment in Tibetan Buddhism is the reason for its other name, Vajrayana—the Way of the Thunderbolt.

All the Buddhist schools see meditation as being central to their religious practice, but each school has its own defining ritual characteristics.

The Gelugpa School's Kalachakra Ceremony

Imagine, if you will, Madison Square Garden filled to overflowing—not an unusual sight, because the Garden is often packed with fight fans or people cheering on their favorite ice hockey team. On the floor of the Garden is not a sports team, but rather one man dressed in brightly colored robes seated on a raised platform. Around him are others dressed only slightly less elegantly and wearing tall, feathered yellow hats.

These people are chanting in a deep bass tone and playing exotic instruments. But this is not some bizarre rock concert; it is the most solemn ritual of the Gelugpa School of Vajrayana (also called Tibetan) Buddhism, the Kalachakra Initiation, and it is being administered by the most revered of Tibetan Buddhist monks, the Dalai Lama.

In front of the Dalai Lama, who is sitting on the raised platform, is a large, complex picture that has been painstakingly crafted out of many different colored sands. This picture might take several weeks to construct because the grains of sand often have to be placed one or two at a time by monk-artists who spend their whole lives mastering the intricate design. This is the Kalachakra Mandala. It represents a sort of road map of the entire universe as it is understood by Vajrayana Buddhists. Its purpose is to help lead the individual to nirvana.

The ritual element of Tibetan Buddhism is particularly evident in the Kalachakra ceremony. Everything in the ceremony is calculated to involve the recipient in the initiation. Rather than deny the body, Tibetan Buddhism believes in using the entire body as a vehicle for salvation.

Sweet-smelling incense, bright colors in intricate patterns, the heavy, rhythmic bass of the instruments, and the massed choir of monks are all used to slowly lead the practitioner's consciousness out of the world of the senses and into higher realms of reality. Here, the mandala is of central importance. Even the material from which the mandala is constructed is symbolic, representing the temporary nature of human existence. At the end of the ritual, the mandala is destroyed and the sand is thrown into the sea or a river, never to be used again. This emphasizes the transient nature of samsara.

Many other symbols are used as well. The Dalai Lama and many of the monks hold *dorjes* and *ghantas* with which they perform ritual hand movements called *mudras*. Dorjes are small double-ended scepters, usually made of bronze, which represent lightning bolts. In turn, these lightning bolts represent both skillful means—that is, the practice of using all facets of the human existence to gain enlightenment—and the indestructible, changeless nature of reality. The ghantas are hand bells and represent the wisdom the practitioner is attempting to cultivate.

What's It All Mean? _____

> **Dorjes** are small double-ended scepters that represent the masculine principle. **Ghantas** are hand bells that represent the feminine principle. When performing the ritual hand movements called **mudras,** the union of these two principles is an enlightened mind.

Other symbols can be found in Tibetan Buddhism. One of these is the *phurba*, or ritual dagger, which is used to symbolically cut off ignorance. Also used in some rituals are cups made from human skulls and trumpets made from human thighbones.

These might seem strange or even repelling to European or American eyes, but this need not be the case. Like all Buddhists, the Tibetans believe that all human beings go through an endless series of rebirths. Thus, death is neither a unique event nor one to be feared. The body that is left behind is of no particular significance. If it is utilized in a good way, its former owner will benefit in his new life from this use.

Bet You Didn't Know

A good example of a strange ritual is *sky burial*. Here, the body of the deceased is cut into pieces and laid out for scavengers. After it has been defleshed, the bones are collected, cleaned, and either buried or used to make religious articles. To the Tibetans, giving your dead body as food to other living creatures and for the making of religious articles is an act of great generosity that benefits all concerned.

Vajrayana Buddhism Celebrations

Rituals and festivals in Vajrayana Buddhism are not tied to the Buddhist year with its recurring religious holidays. The Tibetan calendar is lunar, and the days on which festivals occur can vary quite widely. The Tibetans celebrate the birth of the Buddha on the ninth day of the fourth month of the year. They celebrate his enlightenment and death on the fifteenth day of the fourth month.

On the fourth day of the first month, the Tibetans begin to celebrate *Monlam Chenmo*, which goes on for three weeks. On the fifteenth day of the fifth month, offerings are made to local gods and goddesses who are believed to be the protectors of the Buddhist teachings. Of particular interest to the majority of the Gelugpa School are the festival of the death of its founder Je Tsongkhapa (on the twenty-fifth day of the tenth month) and the birth-day of the present Dalai Lama (on July 6 of the Western calendar).

We've looked at several schools of Buddhism in this and the preceding chapters. In the next chapter, we'll look at one more—Pure Land Buddhism.

The Least You Need to Know

- The essence of Vajrayana training is the perfection of meditation through ritual practice.

- At the abhiseka (initiation ceremony), the student receives his mantra (meditation formula) and the mandala (road map) of his yidam (personal deity).

- The Tibetan School believes an individual can achieve enlightenment in one lifetime—if he is prepared to take certain risks.

- Tibetan Buddhists believe that because people have different talents and abilities, each individual must use a different combination of techniques to leave the cycle of birth and death.

- The most revered monk in the Gelugpa School of Vajrayana (Tibetan) Buddhism is the Dalai Lama.

Pure Land Buddhism

In This Chapter

- Birth of Pure Land Buddhism
- The Dhyani Buddhas
- Pure Land Buddhism progression

All the paths of Buddhism we have discussed up to this point are very difficult for the layperson to practice. They require the practitioner to leave society and spend long hours in meditation or ritual practice to achieve the desired goal of enlightenment.

For the vast majority of people, this is neither an attractive nor a possible alternative to life in the world. Family and social obligations do not allow it. What hope, then, does Buddhism hold for such people? Is supporting monks or engaging in preparatory practices the most they can aspire to? Are they required, in effect, to postpone any hope of enlightenment until a future incarnation? These questions arose early in the history of Buddhism, and the answers that evolved were to give birth to perhaps the most widespread of the Buddhist schools—the Pure Land School.

Rebirth in a Pure Universe

The roots of the Pure Land lie in India. As we saw in Chapter 3, new ideas associated with the Mahayana School started to develop in India sometime around 100 B.C.E. One of these new ideas was the concept that the universe we inhabit was only one of many.

In the Buddhist scriptures, we read that near the end of his life, the Buddha was strolling through the forest one day when he casually mentioned to his attendant Ananda that, if someone should ask him, a Buddha could live on in the world indefinitely. Unfortunately, Ananda was not the quickest of the Buddha's disciples, and he failed to take the hint. Undaunted, the Buddha repeated himself. Again Ananda failed to ask the appropriate question. The Buddha tried one more time. When Ananda still did not ask the Buddha to remain in the world, the Buddha promptly informed Ananda that he would soon die.

For Buddhists, the Buddha's death marks the beginning of the decline in the power of the Buddha's message in our world. As time goes on and we become more distanced from the time of the Buddha, the moral condition of the world continues to decline. Indeed, many Buddhists believe it has declined so much that in the current age it is impossible to reach enlightenment. However, not all world systems are like ours. The main reason for this is that each of these worlds had its own

Buddha, and that the Buddhas who had incarnated in those worlds had not died as the Buddha of our world had.

This came to affect the whole goal of religious practice. For the Theravadins, the decline of this world meant that the most they could aim for was a favorable rebirth in a future time when a new Buddha, Maitreya, will appear on earth to rejuvenate the Buddhist faith. But many Mahayana Buddhists had a more immediate possibility—rebirth in a different, pure universe. These universes came to be known collectively as the Pure Land.

Enlighten Me

Maitreya has been prophesized to appear as the next Buddha, the last of five Buddhas to achieve supreme enlightenment. He will take his last rebirth as a human being on earth, quickly achieve enlightenment, and proclaim the divine law for all to benefit.

The Buddhas who had established Buddhism in these other worlds had been gifted with disciples who were somewhat quicker on the uptake than poor Ananda. Consequently, these Buddhas continue to live forever. As a result, their worlds not only did not decay as our own had, but actually improved to the degree that, from our perspective, they were paradises. In fact, they were so perfect that anyone being born into such a world was inevitably able to progress spiritually to the point that he would achieve enlightenment in the course of one lifetime.

Supernatural Human Allies

The goal of Buddhists in our world, as the Pure Land Buddhists envision it, is to be reborn into one of these Pure Land worlds. However, there is a problem. Pure Land Buddhists believe that our world is so corrupt that nothing we could do on our own would be sufficient to ensure our rebirth in the Pure Land. Fortunately, human beings have "supernatural allies" in the Dhyani Buddhas, the Buddhas who rule the Pure Lands.

The most famous of these Buddhas is Amitabha. Like all Buddhas and Bodhisattvas, Amitabha took a vow that he would save all intelligent beings. In this case, this meant he would aid anyone who called upon him with perfect faith to be reborn in his Pure Land. This would assure that the person would achieve enlightenment in his next life.

In one stroke, this concept breathed new life into Buddhism. Before Pure Land Buddhism, meditation, ritual, and text study could be practiced only by those who could afford the large outlay of time these methods demanded—those who had either renounced the world or were independently wealthy. But the basic tenet of Pure Land, that salvation depended on faith more than on works, meant that common people, tradesmen, and peasants could now enter fully into Buddhist practice.

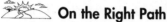 **On the Right Path**

> Amitabha Buddha (Sanskrit) is called Amida-butsu in Japan and also sometimes referred to as Amida Buddha.

There now arose a series of devotional exercises and literature aimed toward the class of people who had, up to now, been more or less relegated to the role of support staff to the monks and nuns. Although the peasants could and did continue to gain merit through giving, they could also aspire to salvation through the aid of supernatural beings.

Through the constant repetition of short formulas and prayers, the lower classes could both work and pray at the same time. This, coupled with pilgrimages to sacred sites whenever possible and the support of the monks, became characteristic of the followers of Pure Land Buddhism.

Pure Land Buddhism Reaches Out

Pure Land never seems to have been a large school in India, but when it spread to East Asia, its progress accelerated rapidly. Part of the reason for this was that both China and Japan produced many gifted preachers. Unfortunately, their championing of the Pure Land doctrine was often seen as subversive by the ecclesiastical and lay authorities, who from time to time persecuted them.

All this only served to reinforce in the minds of the common people the idea that Pure Land Buddhism was the Buddhism of the people, whereas other forms were the Buddhism of the upper class. Consequently, Pure Land Buddhism spread widely throughout the lower strata of society in China and Japan. It is not surprising, therefore, to find that Pure Land Buddhism was the first Buddhism to reach America as people from these classes emigrated in search of a better life.

On the Right Path

> Some differences between (Traditional/ Chinese) Pure Land and (Sinran/Japanese) True Pure Land are as follows: Traditional Pure Land believes a cooperative relationship exists between Amitabha Buddha and the practitioner—the practitioner tries to become one with the purified mind. Shinran True Pure Land believes a person is totally reliant on the primal vow of Amida Buddha—enlightenment is not dependent in any way on one's own efforts.

We've looked at the many schools of Buddhism. Now we'll look at how Buddhism has held up in the ever-changing modern world.

The Least You Need to Know

- A different, pure universe where one can be reborn came to be known collectively as the Pure Land.

- The Dhyani Buddhas are supernatural human allies who continue to live forever in paradises; each of these Buddhas will aid any human who calls upon him with perfect faith to be reborn into his Pure Land.

- The basic tenet of Pure Land—salvation depends on faith more than works—means that common people can enter fully into Buddhist practice.

- Pure Land Buddhism spread throughout the lower strata of society in China and Japan because of the belief that it was the Buddhism of the people, whereas other forms were the Buddhism of the upper class.

Chapter 9

Buddhism and the Challenge of the Modern World

In This Chapter

- Religious strain in Sri Lanka
- Southeast Asia deals with the modern world
- Buddhism in China
- Korea and Japan
- Destruction of the Tibetan culture

Buddhism has had a long and interesting history, but it would be unwise to assume that its glories are all in the past or that it is no longer a dynamic religion. As we shall see in this chapter, Buddhism has been forced to adapt to the swiftly changing conditions of the modern world. In some cases, the transition has gone smoothly. In others, however, the tensions between Buddhism and modern ideologies have not been resolved without severe difficulties.

Buddhism and National Identity in Sri Lanka

Buddhism has had a long history in Sri Lanka. After swiftly becoming an established part of the culture (see Chapter 5), Buddhism continued to solidify its hold on the consciousness of the people (the Sinhalas) for several centuries. Indeed, it was in Sri Lanka that the scriptures of the Theravada School were first committed to writing in the first century B.C.E. It should be noted, however, that other schools of Buddhism flourished there as well. The Theravada School did not become the official religion of Sri Lanka until the time of Parakkama-Bahu, who reigned from 1153 to 1186 C.E.

But it was during this time that the steady progress of Buddhism was interrupted by political upheaval. Sri Lanka began to experience recurring invasions of the northern part of the island by Dravidian-speaking Tamil peoples from South India. These invaders were, by and large, Hindus who felt no compulsion to support the Buddhist religious establishment. As their influence waxed and waned through the centuries, so, too, did the fortunes of Buddhism in Sri Lanka. It is no surprise, then, that Buddhism came to be associated more and more with the Indo-European–speaking Sinhala group, just as Hinduism came to be associated with the Dravidian-speaking Tamils.

This association became explicit during the reign of King Dutugamuna (101 to 88 B.C.E.), when the Sinhala people regained control of much of the

northern section of Sri Lanka that had previously
been violently taken from them by a Tamil invader.
In order to do so, Dutugamuna raised the standard
of religious war, casting the conflict in terms of
righteous Buddhist Sinhalas regaining their homeland from unrighteous Hindu Tamils. This was a
pattern of rhetoric that would be intensified and
consolidated by subsequent kings until it became
an article of faith within Sinhala culture. Thus, a
tension was created that would bear bitter fruit in
Sri Lanka even to the present day.

This pattern was further reinforced with the arrival
of European powers in the early 1600s. Driven by a
mixture of commercial ambition and religious fervor, the European powers were to play an increasingly important role not only in Sri Lanka, but also
throughout all of Asia. The Portuguese were the
first such colonial power in Sri Lanka. Conditioned
by centuries of warfare against the Muslims in the
Iberian Peninsula during the period known as the
Reconquista, the Portuguese came to associate
their colonial expansion with the expansion of their
own austere form of Roman Catholicism.

Fiercely intolerant of all other religious expression,
the Portuguese carried out a vigorous program of
eradicating Buddhist and Hindu religious sites and
of conversion (often forced) to Roman Catholicism.
The Dutch soon displaced the Portuguese and
promptly imposed their own Protestant religious
preferences on the region. They, in turn, were followed by the British, who were primarily interested
in trade and felt that their interests were best
served through a policy of religious tolerance.

Bet You Didn't Know

Even though Buddhism is currently the national religion in Sri Lanka's constitution, Buddhism (70 percent), Hinduism (15 percent), Islam (7 percent), and Christianity (8 percent) are all practiced there. Small numbers of Baha'is can be found as well. The western part of the country has the largest concentration of Christians, and the northern part is almost entirely Hindu. The south has the overwhelming presence of Buddhism, and the rest of the country is a mixture of religions.

As colonial expansion increased, the political power of the Sinhala (and Tamil) peoples decreased until the only indigenous independent state was the kingdom of Kandy in the hilly center of Sri Lanka. It was inevitable, given the religious prejudices exhibited by the invading European colonial powers, that the Kandyan kingdom was perceived as the guardian of Sri Lankan Buddhism. Moreover, Buddhism and political independence came to be intimately linked in the Sri Lankan mind just as it had in years past. This link became very important in the postcolonial period for the direction Buddhism had taken in Sri Lanka.

Sri Lanka's Colonial Period

During the colonial period, Sri Lanka had seen its full share of Christian missionary activity. But the

Buddhist Sangha (Order) had always been able to maintain much of its dominant position. Because most colonial activity was confined to the coastal regions of the island, the kingdom of Kandy, protected from intrusion by its surrounding palisade of mountains, remained a haven for traditional Sri Lankan life and culture, and a lavish supporter of institutional Buddhism. All this changed with the arrival of the British. In 1815, with the threat of French and Dutch ships disrupting their lines of communication with their eastern colonies, the British proceeded to eliminate the Kandyan kingdom.

With the disappearance of this last official protector, the Buddhists found that they now served a new master who did not understand their ancient traditions. At first, this seemed to present no great problem. The British rulers of South Asia had no interest in the religious lives of their subjects. Motivated by the ledger rather than the Bible, they were satisfied if they received their duties and taxes. But events in Great Britain were to change the colonial government's easygoing attitudes toward religion in Sri Lanka.

One of the major causes of this shift of opinion was a wave of evangelical fervor that swept through Great Britain. Many influential people now believed that Britain had a moral responsibility to its colonial subjects. Given the tenor of the times, this meant that every effort should be made to bring the indigenous populations within the fold of Christianity. This left the British colonial government in Sri Lanka (and elsewhere) in a paradoxical position.

On one hand, they believed the indigenous people would indeed be better off as Christians. On the other hand, they were bound by the promises of tolerance they had given religious authorities in Sri Lanka at the time of the Kandyan conquest. Buddhism had become very much a state religion. Its growth in Sri Lanka was such that the king (or the government acting in his stead) held control of the monasteries' financial assets and served as the judge in disputes between the different groups. When the Kandyan kingdom had been dissolved, these functions were taken over by the British, who pledged to support the Buddhist religion, as had its native predecessor.

But as the clamor for increased missionary activity in Sri Lanka increased, the colonial government found it harder and harder to fulfill this pledge. When the older generation of sympathetic administrators died or retired, their replacements felt less and less bound to honor this obligation.

Peaceful Coexistence Becomes Strained

By 1840, missionary activity was in full swing. By 1860, with the aid of the government, Buddhism was being forced more and more on the defensive. It is not surprising, therefore, that during this period we see a change in Buddhist attitudes away from peaceful coexistence with the Christians and toward a confrontational counterattack on the missionaries and their religion.

The initial drive for this came from a rather peculiar source. Colonial Henry Olcott was an

American Civil War hero who had become a follower of H. P. Blavatsky and one of the founders of a new religious movement called Theosophy, which incorporated into itself many ideas taken from Hinduism and Buddhism. Convinced of the spiritual value of Eastern thought, Olcott sailed to India and Sri Lanka in 1880 to study it in its natural environment.

Appalled by the actions the Christian missionaries were taking in Sri Lanka, Olcott launched a successful campaign to organize Buddhist opposition to the new religion. This included the foundation of lay Buddhist organizations, Buddhist schools, and an organized refutation of the Christian missionary position. In due time, he passed the torch to his protégé, David Hewavitarne, who is better known to history by his religious name—Anagarika Dharmapala (1864–1933).

Bet You Didn't Know

Madame H. P. Blavatsky was born in Russia in 1831 and died in England in 1891. She launched the Theosophical Movement, calling her message Theosophy. She introduced knowledge of eastern religions to the West—including the ideas of karma and reincarnation.

Dharmapala did more to revitalize Sri Lankan Buddhism than any other single person in modern history, and his efforts didn't stop at the coast of

Sri Lanka. Deeply distressed by the fact that the Buddhist holy places in Northern India were in the hands of Hindus, he organized the formation of the Maha Bodhi Society to purchase and refurbish them. In the process, the sites once again became centers of pilgrimage for Buddhists from all over the world. This marked the beginning of the revival of Buddhism in the land of its birth.

 Bet You Didn't Know _____

Dharmapala never became a monk of the Buddhist Order despite living like one all his life. In Sri Lanka, he began to support the formation of lay Buddhist groups for the practice of meditation. Buddhist meditation had traditionally been the preserve of the monks, so this new trend toward lay involvement in religion brought Buddhism more and more into the public arena.

As the agitation for political freedom escalated, it became apparent to the politicians that Buddhism still greatly influenced the Sinhalese peasant population. A good example of how far they were willing to go to exploit this can be seen in the career of S.W.R.D. Bandaranaike.

Bandaranaike had been raised an Anglican, but he adopted the religion of his ancestors as a useful adjunct to his rising civil service career. Bandaranaike had even proposed before Sri Lankan independence that the proper language for studying Buddhism was not Pali or Sinhalese (the language of the majority of the population), but English! However, sometime between then and his election as prime minister in 1956 he had become a born-again Buddhist.

It was at this point that he and others like him came to present Buddhist as the normative religion of Sri Lanka. Needless to say, this did not sit well with the more than 20 percent of the island's people who were not Buddhist. The Christians, and to a far greater degree, the Hindu Tamil speakers of the north and northeastern parts of the island, found themselves increasingly politically isolated as politicians exploited sectarian differences.

With this increased emphasis on religious differences, rioting broke out as the government began a deliberate shift toward isolationist policies. The legislation that began to be passed disenfranchised English in favor of Sinhalese, abolished the state-mandated quotas that guaranteed the Tamils a significant share in educational institutions and the government, and started to promote Buddhism at the expense of other religions.

The results are still with us. Sri Lanka has suffered for more than a decade with a smoldering and bitter civil war that has often been waged through the appeal of both sides to religious principles. Not only does the government periodically mount military operations against Hindu strongholds in the northern and eastern parts of the island, but the Hindus also retaliate with a campaign of terrorism in the Sinhalese-held parts of Sri Lanka.

The tragedy of Sri Lanka is that Buddhism, one of the world's most peaceful religions, has become a rallying point for violence and intolerance. Sadly, this is the case not only in Sri Lanka, but elsewhere in the Buddhist world as well. We can see similar forces at work in Southeast Asia.

Buddhism and Colonialism in Southeast Asia

For many years, the countries now known as Indonesia, the Philippines, Malaysia, Vietnam, Cambodia, Thailand, Laos, and Burma (known as Myanmar since 1989) had been influenced by cultural currents emanating from India and, to a somewhat lesser extent, China. A number of historians in the earlier part of the twentieth century saw Buddhism (and Hinduism) as being carried into Southeast Asia on a wave of cultural imperialism.

Although it is true that the indigenous cultures of the region found these religions and other aspects of Indian and Chinese culture appealing and incorporated them into their own cultural traditions, it would be unwise to see this as a naive acceptance or one resulting from outside pressure. These cultures appear to have absorbed these new religious forms on their own terms, and they seem to have modified these new traditions in such a manner as to have them become, for all intents and purposes, indigenous religions in their own right.

Buddhism presents a good example of this. Chinese records show that Buddhism was established on the coast of Vietnam at a very early period, but the exact dates of its arrival in the region are unknown. Yet it might very well be that it was from Vietnam, as well as from Central Asia, that Buddhism first penetrated China. In any event, it is clear that Buddhism and Hinduism traveled along the maritime trade routes to Southeast Asia at a very early date, probably starting in the second century B.C.E.

Bet You Didn't Know

Legend has it that Asoka (one of India's greatest rulers and a supporter of the Buddhist Sangha) sent two missionaries into Burma in the third century B.C.E. Although no corroborating evidence in Burma substantiates this claim, the nearness of Burma to the centers of Mauryan power makes such a claim very possible. If this is the case, this likely marks the first penetration of Buddhism into Southeast Asia.

It was Hinduism that first attracted royal patronage in Southeast Asia, and it is for this reason that we have very little archaeological evidence to trace the development of Buddhism here. All this changes around 1000 C.E., though. After this date, Buddhism increasingly became the official religion of the growing nation-states of Southeast Asia. In these areas, the more conservative Theravadin School based on the Sri Lankan model was the form of choice. By c. 1300 C.E., Burma, Thailand, Laos, and Cambodia had become Theravada Buddhist countries.

The practice of linking Buddhism with the state, which had come to be a distinctive feature of Sri Lankan Buddhism, was widespread in Southeast Asia as well, partially as a result of local conditions and partially due to the fact that Buddhist leaders in this area saw Sri Lanka as the senior center of their religion. In any case, Buddhism flourished and was nurtured by royal patronage.

 Bet You Didn't Know

Indonesia's indigenous religion, which combined the worship of Shiva and the Buddha, began to fall more and more under the sway of Islam. The Philippines seemed to have been content to practice their various indigenous religions. Vietnam chose to follow a form of Mahayana Buddhism closely linked to China.

Enter the European Powers

The practice of linking Buddhism with the state changed as the European powers extended their influence over the region. This was, however, a relatively late development. The earliest colonizers, the Portuguese and the Spanish who came to

Southeast Asia in the late fifteenth century, did not attempt to totally dominate the region at first. They were satisfied with controlling the relatively small areas around their trading ports. Thus, despite the fact that they saw colonization and religious conversion as the same thing, they only affected small areas of the Philippines and Indonesia.

More concerted were the nineteenth-century efforts of the Dutch in Indonesia; the French in Vietnam, Cambodia, and Laos; and the British in Burma, Malaysia, and Singapore.

The first area to receive the unwelcome attention of the Europeans was Burma. In an escalating series of wars, the British progressively incorporated more and more of Burma into their Indian empire. By 1880, the old state of Burma had effectively ceased to exist.

The French began their colonial efforts in Southeast Asia at about the same time. Supposedly, in order to protect Roman Catholic missionaries in Vietnam, the French began a series of aggressive wars that gobbled up more and more Vietnamese territory. Although they tolerated the existence of a Vietnamese emperor up to 1954, by 1900 the French controlled not only Vietnam, but Cambodia and Laos as well. Thus, the only part of Buddhist Southeast Asia that remained independent was Thailand, and this was only because neither the British to the west nor the French to the east would allow the other to possess it. As in Sri Lanka, Buddhism in Thailand came to be intimately linked with the concept of nationhood in the popular mind and would play a role in the region's fight to regain its independence. The situation in mainland Southeast Asia displayed a number of similarities with that of Sri Lanka.

Burma and the Modern World

In Burma (Myanmar), Theravada Buddhism was the religious faith of the Burman ethnic group, which made up some 75 percent of the total population of the country. It is not surprising, therefore, that the struggle to escape the colonial grasp of Great Britain was, to some degree, associated with the resurgence of Buddhism in the same way it had been in Sri Lanka.

Bet You Didn't Know

Vipassana is an ancient meditation technique. It is a way of transforming oneself by observing oneself, the highest form of awareness. The Buddha is said to have practiced Vipassana meditation when he discovered the path of the "middle way" in all things. This technique is considered so valuable that in Burma it was preserved precisely as it began, more than 2,200 years ago.

In 1906, the Young Men's Buddhist Association was formed. This organization provided the leadership that would win the country independence in 1948. But the Burma that was created at this time was by

no means a monolithic Burman state. Some 25 percent of its population was of different ethnic back-
grounds, and many of these people had been
heavily influenced by European missionaries and
become Christian.

It is not difficult to understand why these con-
stituent groups of the Burman state were hesitant
to support any institution that would bolster
Buddhist domination. Their fears were not decreased by the appointment of U Nu as prime minister of the new Burmese Federation. U Nu was a
pious Buddhist to whom being Burmese and being
Buddhist were identical. His vision of Burma's
future was one associated with a sort of Buddhist
Socialism. This led to an insurrection of the
Karens, who were mostly Christian and wanted
their own state. Early Karen victories in the early
1950s led to the appointment of Ne Win as the
commander of the government forces. This was to
be a momentous appointment.

Meanwhile, U Nu sponsored a Buddhist religious
revival in the hope of promoting unity in the
country. In 1956, Burma hosted an international
conference of Buddhist luminaries to celebrate the
2,500th birthday of the Buddha. This did not
calm the anxiety of the minority groups who feared
Burman domination, and these groups, who tended
to live in the mountainous marginal land that
surrounded the fertile rice-producing river valleys,
increasingly sought to gain autonomy from the
central government. This, in turn, drove the government to place more and more power in the
hands of the military.

In 1958, the military, under the command of General Ne Win, took control of the country. An unsuccessful attempt was made to return to civilian rule in 1960. It was at this time that the Burmese constitution was amended to make Buddhism the official religion of the country. But civilian government proved once again ineffectual, and in 1962 the military, let by Ne Win, took up the reins of power once more—where they have remained to the present day.

At the same time, the military closed off Burma from interaction with the rest of the world. Except for brief periods of relative openness, Burma still remains one of the most isolated countries on earth. The resulting political climate has been one of unremitting oppression. All critics of the regime have been silenced either by intimidation or assassination.

The Buddhist monks haven't been exempt from this type of treatment. Consequently, the state-supported Buddhist Order has become little more than a government department. On the other hand, many dissident monks have joined resistance groups that oppose the government and are very active in the struggle to return Burma to a democratic system of government.

Vietnam and the Modern World

The Buddhist relationship to the state was one of the key factors in the recent history of Vietnam as well, but in a somewhat different fashion. When the French gained control of the areas now known as Vietnam, Cambodia, and Laos in the late nineteenth century, they realized they were going to need indigenous personnel in their administration. To fill those positions, they turned to the relatively small number of Vietnamese who had converted to Christianity.

When the region gained its independence, it was natural that the government would be turned over to individuals with the experience to run it. Thus, the Roman Catholic Vietnamese, who represented no more than 10 percent of the population, came to control the lives of the much more numerous Buddhists.

In time, the Buddhists, under the direction of activist monks, began to demonstrate for a restoration of Buddhist civil rights. The Catholic minority tried to hold on to power, but after a series of spectacular martyrdoms in which Buddhist monks calmly poured gasoline over their bodies and burned themselves to death, the Catholic government was deposed.

Subsequent events, such as the Indo-Chinese wars and the Communist takeover of Vietnam, curtailed but did not completely suppress Buddhism. Despite repression by the Communist government of Vietnam, the religion is still very much in evidence both in Vietnam and among the immigrant communities of Europe and the United States.

On the Right Path

> Thich Nhat Hanh is a Vietnamese Buddhist monk who worked for reconciliation between North and South Vietnam during the war in Vietnam. Martin Luther King Jr. nominated him for the Nobel Peace Prize in 1967.

Cambodia and the Modern World

Buddhism had been an honored part of Cambodian life for many centuries when Cambodia resumed its independence in 1953. But in 1975, it suffered a blow from which it still has not recovered. In that year, the new masters of Cambodia, the Khmer Rouge, decided that in order to renovate Cambodian society, they were going to eliminate all elements of society that did not lead directly to a socialist state.

They proceeded to deport to the countryside and kill many of the country's educated elite—which included most Buddhist monks. In a brief reign of terror, some 15 centuries of Buddhist culture were almost completely eradicated. Only a few monks managed to flee the country in time. As a result, Cambodian Buddhist culture was kept alive by a handful of monks in such diverse places as Long Beach, California; Lowell, Massachusetts; and Paris, France.

On the Right Path

Buddhism resumed a central role in Cambodian social and political life with the establishment of a legitimate Cambodian government in 1993.

Today, attempts are being made to renovate Cambodian Buddhism in its homeland, but so much tradition has been lost and destroyed that it is questionable whether it will ever be restored to its former grandeur.

State Persecution of Buddhism in China

In China, the situation was somewhat different. Despite Buddhism's great initial successes, the Confucian ruling class, which continued to dominate the Chinese government, always found it suspect. Buddhism, as they saw it, undermined traditional Chinese family values, and donations to the various Chinese schools of Buddhism reduced the tax base. It is not surprising, therefore, that Buddhism was periodically persecuted in China. As time when on, these persecutions took their toll.

Among the peasants, Buddhism continued to command a faithful following, more so on the strength of its supposed magical potency than because of a deep devotion to its metaphysical principles. Consequently, when the Chinese reasserted themselves politically, they did so intellectually as well. New forms of Confucianism came to dominate Chinese thinking. Buddhism became more and more a rural religion practiced by the politically disenfranchised, and it never regained the intellectual stature it had enjoyed in the seventh and eighth centuries C.E.

But it would be unwise to conclude from this that Chinese Buddhist philosophical thought disappeared entirely. China's efforts to exclude foreign invaders and to reestablish its political unity drew a number of young monks into a struggle for modernity. Although they were never a majority of the Sangha and were often disapproved of by the official leaders of the Buddhist community, they were to have an effect on the modern development of Buddhism in China.

The most famous of these monks was T'ai-hsu (1890–1947). He founded schools, promoted the study of Buddhist languages other than Chinese, and advocated the idea of a world federation of Buddhists. These efforts were just beginning to bear fruit when China was taken over by the Communists, who saw the Buddhist monks and nuns as parasites who were draining the vitality of the Chinese people.

In 1951, the Communists confiscated most of the monastic lands and returned young monks and nuns to the lay state. In 1953, the Chinese Buddhist Association was formed to bring the Buddhist community under government control. Periodic campaigns of repression such as the Red Guard movement further weakened Buddhism in China. Although Buddhism has lost much of its

strength as a result of these persecutions, it still
persists in China and will likely continue to do so
in the foreseeable future.

Bet You Didn't Know

> The Communists believe that Buddhism
> was the spiritual weapon used throughout
> China's history by the ruling class to sup-
> press the lower classes. They also claim
> that because Buddhism teaches about the
> blessings and bliss in a future paradise, it
> keeps people from improving their earthly
> status.

Buddhism in Modern Korea and Japan

Buddhism in Korea and Japan has been closely linked
for many centuries. Indeed, it was often Buddhist
monks from Korea who provided the link between
Chinese and Japanese cultures. By 1000 C.E., Son, a
school of Zen Buddhism, had become the most popular form of Buddhism in Korea. Unfortunately,
Buddhism was repressed by the rigidly Confucian Yi
dynasty of kings (1393–1910). Strangely enough, it
was the Japanese conquest of Korea in 1910 that
marked the revival of Buddhist fortunes.

Although the Japanese allowed a resurgence of
Buddhism in Korea, they attempted to force its

development along Japanese models that were often quite different from indigenous Korean ones. This led to friction that eventually resulted in the formation of a unified Korean Buddhism in 1935. After World War II (1939–1945) and the Korean War (1950–1953), Buddhism was effectively eliminated in North Korea and to some extent curtailed in South Korea. However, Korean Buddhism continues to prosper despite these difficulties not only at home, but abroad as well.

Buddhism in Japan was to have its own share of difficulties in the modern period. During the period after the Meiji Restoration of 1868, Buddhism was ignored in favor of the state-supported Shinto that glorified the emperor. It was during this period that Buddhist clerical celibacy was made illegal. Thus, today, Japanese Buddhism is one of the few forms of Buddhism that allows a married clergy. It was during this period as well that Japanese Buddhism adopted many innovations from the West such as Sunday School, meditation clubs, young people's organizations, and, in some cases, the outward trappings of Protestant ritual and dress.

Bet You Didn't Know

Although 66 percent of Japanese don't consider themselves to be religious, more than 90 percent of Japanese funerals are conducted according to Buddhist rites.

Another interesting development in modern Japanese Buddhism has been the rise of new lay Buddhist organizations such as Soka Gakkai and Rissho-kodeikai. These new organizations have done away with the old organizational principles of Buddhism and replaced them with aggressively new methods that more traditional Buddhists find somewhat upsetting.

On the whole, Japanese Buddhism has become a dynamic part of the national life. Moreover, a number of Japanese schools are finding fertile ground in Europe and America for their ideas and practices.

Buddhism and the Destruction of a Culture in Tibet

For many centuries, Tibet was viewed by China as a province of the Chinese empire. Satisfied with formal submission and the ritual exchange of gifts, China was content to allow the country to be governed by the great monastic orders as it had been for many centuries. All of this changed, however, when the Communists came to power in 1950.

Dissatisfied with the traditional arrangements and anxious to secure its borders, the new Chinese government attempted to rule more directly. To do this, staying consistent with their own atheistic ideology, they occupied the country, suppressed the monasteries, and disenfranchised the Buddhist religion.

In 1959, the Tibetan people rebelled. It was at this time that the present Dalai Lama fled Tibet and settled in India. The Chinese then embarked on a reign of terror designed to completely eradicate Tibetan Buddhism. Temples were looted, monasteries razed, monks tortured and killed, and scriptures burned. But extinguishing the Buddhist faith in Tibet proved to be more difficult than the Chinese Communists imagined.

Monks began to make the long trek across the Himalayas into India, carrying with them the invaluable texts of their faith. As they gathered in India, they reconstituted the ruined monastic colleges and began to teach a new generation of young novices the complex rites and rituals of Tibetan Buddhism.

Meanwhile, the Dalai Lama has become an eloquent and charismatic spokesman for his country and his faith. By bringing his country's difficulties to the world's attention, he has helped popularize Tibetan Buddhism. Many Westerners, attracted by the bright and vibrant nature of the tradition, have begun to support Tibetan efforts to preserve their cultural heritage.

Although the politics of the Chinese occupation of Tibet have yet to be resolved, it can be safely said that Tibetan Buddhism has managed to weather the storm. Through the courage and persistence of present-day practitioners, it will be preserved and passed on intact to future generations.

In the next chapter, we'll look at how each of the schools of Buddhism arrived in the West (Europe and the United States) and got their start.

The Least You Need to Know

- Sri Lanka has suffered for more than a decade with a smoldering and bitter civil war that has often been waged through the appeal of both sides to religious principles.

- Burma remains one of the most isolated countries on earth because of the political climate of unremitting oppression.

- Despite repression by the Communist government, Buddhism is still very much evident in Vietnam.

- Today, attempts are being made to renovate Cambodian Buddhism in its homeland.

- Though Buddhism lost much of its strength to the persecutions in China, it still persists.

- Even with the Communist takeover in North Korea (and the curtailment of Buddhism in South Korea), Korean Buddhism continues to prosper. In addition, Japanese Buddhism has become a dynamic part of the national life.

- Because the Chinese government suppressed the monasteries and disenfranchised the Buddhist religion, the Tibetan people rebelled in 1959, causing the present Dalai Lama to flee Tibet and settle in India.

Buddhism in Europe and the United States

In This Chapter

- Early Western Buddhist appreciation
- Japanese, Chinese, and Korean Zen arrive
- Theravada Buddhism returns
- Vajrayana (Tibetan) Buddhism enters
- Pure Land Buddhism

Buddhism is so much a part of modern culture, at least on a superficial level, it is hard to imagine that only 200 years ago people in the West had almost no idea this religion even existed. Let's look at how each of the schools of Buddhism arrived in the West and got its start.

Early Enthusiasts in the West

Not until the European powers began to carve out their colonial empires in South and Southeast Asia while meddling in the affairs of the East Asian nations did they began to pay attention to the indigenous belief systems of the conquered peoples. But generally this attention had little or nothing to do with the intrinsic worth of these systems. Rather, these early administrators saw religion as a means of social control.

As time progressed, however, some Europeans came to appreciate Buddhism and the other Asian religions in their own right. As they began to master the classical languages of Asia, such as Sanskrit, Chinese, Japanese, and Pali, European scholars began to piece together what was to them a new and fascinating universe of thought. This group of scholars tended to emerge from the lower ranks of the colonial administrators who spent most of their time dealing with the administrative problems of the common people over whom they ruled. Because they had very few other Europeans to socialize with, these officers often took up study of the local culture.

The next major change in Buddhist-European relations came in 1879, when Sir Edwin Arnold published his famous epic poem, *The Light of Asia*. It was a retelling in English verse of the life of the Buddha and not from an academic standpoint, but from that of someone who appreciated Buddhist teaching as religious expression. Soon after this, Helena P. Blavatsky, a Russian, and Henry Steele Olcott, an American, two founders of the religious movement known as Theosophy, traveled to India and Sri Lanka to study Eastern thought. In Sri Lanka, they participated in a ceremony that formally accepted them into the Buddhist faith. Although their understanding of Buddhism was somewhat peculiar, these new converts were enthusiastic.

Bet You Didn't Know

T. W. Rhys-Davids (1843–1922), an administrator in Sri Lanka, spent his leisure hours learning Pali, the sacred language of Theravada Buddhism. What he found astonished him. The Buddhism that began to emerge from the texts was not the (seemingly) superstitious religion that surrounded him, but rather an elegant, subtle philosophy that resonated with the logical, scientific thought that was beginning to dominate European thinking. He became so enthusiastic about his studies that he founded the Pali Text Society with the intention of editing the entire Pali canon and translating it into English.

But the Theosophists were on the tip of an iceberg, so to speak. From around 1850 onward, Europe and the United States began to enter a period of religious crisis. Increasingly, intellectuals (and those who fancied themselves intellectuals) were becoming dissatisfied with Christianity. Some took issue with the origins of humanity and the physical world. Others took issue with Christian claims to the exclusive possession of the means for salvation in this world and the next. Many others simply wanted to replace what they thought of as mere superstition with a more scientific worldview. For many, Buddhism's "sudden" appearance on the intellectual horizon offered an answer to their dilemma.

But these early enthusiasts in Europe and the United States tended to misunderstand Buddhism. As we have seen, Buddhism does not suggest that beings more powerful than humans do not exist. Rather, it simply asserts that their influence is limited and that *ultimate* salvation lies elsewhere. Early European and American adherents to Buddhism tended to interpret Buddhism as being completely atheistic and self-oriented. This was certainly not the case for many, if not most, Buddhists.

It is not surprising, therefore, that early converts to Buddhism tended to lean toward Theravada Buddhism, in which "supernatural" elements seem to be the least pronounced. When Europeans began to investigate Buddhism seriously in the middle of the nineteenth century, they were very attracted to the Pali scriptures of this school of Buddhism because they saw modern European thinking embodied in these ancient works.

As we have seen, this is not precisely the way Theravada Buddhism has been viewed in its indigenous setting. But this early European viewpoint has just enough truth in it to have made Theravada Buddhism an attractive option to many European and U.S. seekers who could not accept an otherworldly component to their spiritual quest.

On the Right Path

The first convert to actually be ordained as a Buddhist monk was Allen Bennett (1872–1925), who was ordained in Burma. He was soon followed by a number of other Britons and Germans who embraced the monastic lifestyle. But it was not until after World War II that the other forms of Buddhism began to make their way into European and American society.

Japanese Zen Arrives

Zen came to the United States with the attendance of the Japanese monk Soyen Shaku (1859–1919) at the great World Parliament of Religions held in Chicago in 1893. Meeting there with Paul Carus, the enthusiastic publisher of religious materials, Shaku agreed to send one of his disciples to help Carus with the translation of Japanese Zen Buddhist texts. This disciple, D. T. Suzuki (1870–1966), was to spend much of his life introducing Zen to the West. Other Zen masters were to follow Suzuki to the United States in the period before World War II, and they soon gathered small groups of enthusiastic American disciples.

World War II itself was a major contributing factor to the new renaissance of European and U.S. interest in Buddhism. The war brought Europeans and Americans into contact with other Buddhist countries such as China and Japan. Buddhist emigrants from these countries had already made a small beachhead in Hawaii and the West Coast of the United States. Unfortunately, racism tended to keep these communities separated from mainstream American life. All this changed after the war.

It was the Beat Generation that emerged, taking Zen to its heart. Writers from this movement such as Jack Kerouac, Gary Snyder, and Allen Ginsberg became ardent publicists for Zen (at least Zen as they understood it). Alan Watts (1915–1973), a wandering jack-of-all-religions, preached the gospel of Zen to an appreciative audience of youthful enthusiasts (mainly in California) during the late 1950s and 1960s. He also wrote numerous books about Zen Buddhism.

Enlighten Me

The essence of Zen training is the perfection of meditation through self-discipline.

This initial groundwork led to an influx of Zen teachers into the United States in the decades that followed. These teachers established Zen training facilities that taught Zen in the old-fashioned, rigorous Japanese manner. Although something of a shock to the first generation of seekers who saw Zen as a "do your own thing" sort of religion, the Zen currently in the United States has, as a result of this second wave of teachers, come more in line with traditional expressions of the religion. Indeed, a number of Americans have been recognized as Zen masters in their own right. It might even be said that a new type of Zen, American Zen, is emerging under their guidance.

Chinese and Korean Zen Arrive

The contributions of the Chinese and Korean Zen schools should not be forgotten. In California, Zen Master Hsuan Hua (1908–) founded the Sino-American Buddhist Association and the Gold Mountain Dhyana Monastery, where the training is very traditional and very rigorous. Other teachers, such as Sheng Yen Chang, are also spreading the teachings of Chinese Zen to America.

Likewise, Korean masters such as Soen Sa Nim (1927–) are revealing the treasures of the lesser-known Korean tradition. Soen Sa Nim established the increasingly popular Kwan Um School (named for Kuan-yin, the Bodhisattva of compassion) in 1972. Samu Sunim preceded him in 1967 with his Toronto-based Zen Lotus Society.

Enter the Real Theravada Buddhism

Just as World War II marked the beginning of Zen's penetration into America, the Indochinese wars of the late 1960s and 1970s marked the beginning of a new appreciation of Theravada Buddhism. During this period, American armed forces serving in Vietnam used the neighboring country of Thailand as a rest and recreation spot. There they came into contact with Theravada Buddhism. Likewise, the increased U.S. presence in Southeast Asia led to a growing number of Peace Corps volunteers being sent to the most stable countries in the region. All this resulted in a heightened awareness of Theravada Buddhism.

Also at this time, a number of people, such as the American meditation teachers Jack Kornfield and Joel Goldstein, went to these countries and to Sri Lanka to study and even be ordained as Buddhist monks under such great contemporary Theravadin teachers as Ajahn Chah in Thailand and Taungpulu Sayadaw in Burma. Eventually, many of them returned to Europe and the United States, either to reenter lay life or to teach as ordained monks. The Theravada Buddhism they taught, however, was somewhat different in nature from that of the countries in which they had trained. There, laypersons did not, by and large, meditate—that was something done by monks. But in the United States and Europe, meditation was to become the primary religious activity of monks and laypersons alike.

Enlighten Me

The essence of Theravada training is the perfection of meditation through monastic regulations and the knowledge of the Pali scriptures.

On the other hand, many traditional lay activities associated with Theravada Buddhism in its homeland did not find a home among Europeans or Americans. The people most drawn to Theravada Buddhism were often those who were not comfortable with traditional religion, particularly its institutional and supernatural aspects.

Just as had been the case earlier in the century, it was the perception of Theravada Buddhism as an atheistic and scientific philosophy—rather than a religion in the traditional sense of the term—that was attractive to this new set of followers. As a consequence, these practitioners did not adopt many of the more devotional aspects of Theravada Buddhism.

Vajrayana (Tibetan) Buddhism Arrives

For many people, the austere meditative practices of the Zen and Theravada varieties were unappealing. These people were looking for a more colorful Buddhism than these traditions provided. The answer to their search for religious meaning lay in Vajrayana Buddhism. This form of Buddhist expression was the least known of the Buddhist schools and the last one to come to the West. Content to remain isolated in its Tibetan homeland, Vajrayana Buddhism might have remained unappreciated by outsiders had it not been for the national catastrophe that overtook it in 1950 (see the "Buddhism and the Destruction of a Culture in Tibet" section in Chapter 9).

The Tibetan monks who left Tibet for India were immediately faced with severe problems. The

Chinese were systematically destroying their entire religious culture. Horrible stories emerged, most of which are, unfortunately, all too true. They told of monasteries burned, monks tortured and killed, and priceless works of art smashed. These activities became even more pronounced in the late 1960s during the Chinese Cultural Revolution. The Tibetan monks needed to find a way to preserve their cultural tradition. Replacing their depleted numbers was no real problem. Tibetans continued to enter the religious life, as many still do today. But how to support these monks now that the great Tibetan monasteries and their holdings were gone was the question. What could be done to replace their texts, many of which were unique to the Tibetan tradition? The answer, the Tibetans swiftly discovered, lay in the West.

Thus, in the 1960s, Tibetan monks began to teach in the West. The most famous of these early missionaries was Chögyam Trungpa (1939–), a tulku of the Kagyu order. He established Samye Ling, the first Tibetan monastery outside Asia, in Dumfriesshire, Scotland, in 1967. From this humble beginning, Trungpa created the far-flung Vajradhatu organization dedicated to propagating Kagyu Tibetan Buddhism in the West.

Enlighten Me

The essence of Vajrayana training is the perfection of meditation through ritual practice.

The more widespread Gelugpa School was somewhat slower in sending out feelers to Europe and the United States. The first teachers of this school who gained disciples in the West were Thubten Yeshe (1935–1984) and his disciple Zopa Rimpoche (1946–), who started the Foundation for the Preservation of the Mahayana Tradition in 1971 and Wisdom Publications, a well-respected publishing house now based in Boston.

But it was in the United States that Tibetan Buddhism really flourished. In 1951, a group of Kalmyks, followers of Tibetan Buddhism for many centuries, were allowed to settle in New Jersey after fleeing from their former homes in postwar Russia. It was here that the first Tibetan Buddhist temple in the United States was established, presided over by the Gelugpa monk Geshe Wangal (1901–1983). This led to the first formal teaching of Tibetan Buddhism in the United States. In 1967, Geshe Wangal's disciple, Geshe Sopa (1923–), was invited by the great Canadian Buddhologist Richard Robinson to join the faculty of the newly established Buddhist Studies Program at the University of Wisconsin. Geshe Sopa, in turn, arranged for the Dalai Lama to come to the United States in 1981, and in that year the Dalai Lama presided over a Kalachakra Initiation, which some 12,000 people were said to have attended.

In 1970, Chögyam Trungpa, wearied by constant internal struggles in his Scottish organization, migrated to the United States. At Boulder, Colorado, he established a new international

Vajradhatu organization. He was succeeded as head of this organization by his American disciple Osel Tendzin (1945–1990). More orthodox in his approach was the Gelugpa master Kalu Rinpoche (1905–1989), whose saintly personality and rigorous traditional approach to Tibetan Buddhist training produced the first group of authentically trained Western Vajrayana monks qualified to run their own training establishments.

It was in the United States as well that *Nyingma* Tibetan Buddhism found a new lease of life. In 1969, Tarthang Tulku established the Tibetan Nyingma Institute in Berkley, California. He was soon followed by other notable teachers of the school, including its supreme head, Dudjom Rinpoche (1904–1987). One of Tarthang Tulku's major projects was to edit and publish the enormous corpus of Nyingma scriptures. This, along with other similar ventures such as Wisdom Publications (a publisher of Buddhist books), has ensured that the immensely rich scriptural tradition of Tibetan Buddhism will be preserved for future generations.

What's It All Mean?

> When new tantras were brought to Tibet from India in the twelfth century, individuals who preserved the original tantric texts and ancestry became known as **Nyingma,** or ancient ones, and those who followed the new tantras became known as Sarma, the new tradition.

Pure Land Arrives

The Pure Land Buddhism school has been part of the American scene since the mid-nineteenth century, when Chinese and Japanese workmen were brought to the United States to work on the railroads and in the cane fields of Hawaii. Over the years, it has acquired many trappings reminiscent of Protestant Christianity not only in the West, but even in the lands of its birth.

By and large, Pure Land Buddhism has remained in the Asian community. Most non-Asians who are attracted to Buddhism are drawn to the radical difference of its core message from that of Christianity and Judaism. Thus Pure Land Buddhism, with its many apparent similarities to these traditions (see Chapter 8), does not seem as appealing as the more exotic forms of Buddhism. Nevertheless, its traditional followers are still numerous, particularly the Japanese school of Jodo Shin-shu, under the title of the Buddhist Churches of America (founded in 1899).

In the next chapter, we'll look at Buddhism in the twenty-first century and how it applies to the challenges of a new century.

The Least You Need to Know

- The relationship between Buddhism and the West changed when Westerners began studying Buddhist culture and learned to appreciate its teachings as religious expression.

- The first of the great Buddhist invasions of North America was the Zen craze that swept through America during the 1950s and 1960s and included Japanese, Chinese, and Korean Zen.

- When Theravada Buddhism arrived in the West for the second time, it again had the perception of an atheistic and scientific philosophy; this time it was attractive to a new set of followers.

- Vajrayana (Tibetan) Buddhism flourished in the United States because people were looking for a more colorful Buddhism than the austere meditative practices of Zen and Theravada.

- Pure Land Buddhism has acquired many similarities with Protestant Christianity not only in the West, but also in the lands of its birth. This appeals to some, yet not to all.

Buddhism in the Twenty-First Century

In This Chapter

- Tackling environmental and social issues
- Opportunities for women
- Individual actions and ritual
- A message of hope, peace, and compassion

Buddhism is no different from other world religions in that it faces challenges as well as opportunities in the modern world. In this chapter, we'll look at how Buddhism uses nonviolent and innovative techniques to tackle those challenges, and how it applies compassion and understanding to create opportunities. In addition, we'll see the unique ways Buddhism has come to appeal to many individuals in Western society.

Facing the Challenges of a Changing World

The twentieth century was not kind to Buddhism. Large areas of the Buddhist world disappeared due to political and social changes. A good example of this is China (see Chapter 9), where Buddhism had once been widespread. After the Communists took power, Buddhism was so systematically suppressed (along with all other religions) that it is difficult today to discern how many Buddhists still remain in that huge country.

As we have seen, the Communists carried their suppression of Buddhism to Tibet in 1951 where they attempted to stamp out Buddhism entirely, often by extraordinarily violent means. Likewise, during the hideous excesses of the Khmer Rouge in Cambodia between 1975 and 1979, virtually the entire Buddhist Monastic Order was murdered along with perhaps as much as half of the entire population of this Theravadin Buddhist country. Many estimate that by the end of this period, out of an initial 80,000 monks, only a few hundred managed to survive.

 Bet You Didn't Know _____

> In addition to the human atrocities of the Khmer Rouge, numerous temples in China, Cambodia, and Tibet were destroyed, scriptures burned, and valuable pieces of Buddhist art sold to the highest bidder.

Terrible as this overt attempt to destroy Buddhism has been, it is eclipsed by a more concerted and subtle assault on the religion through the medium of Western culture. Smuggled in on the backs of Mickey Mouse and Michael Jackson, the Western gospel of consumerism is entirely at odds with Buddhist values that preach simplicity, tranquility, and turning away from the relentless acquisitions of goods. But the Coca-Colonization of Asian societies has left them awash in rock videos, Western night-clubs, and expensive electronic consumer goods. Although certainly not bad in themselves, these things provide a not-so-subtle counterpoint to the traditional Buddhist values of simplicity and disen-gagement with the world of the senses.

These Western capitalist forces have created this counterpoint by attempting to replace Buddhist ideals with their own vision of the nature of human happiness as the pursuit of "stuff": the idea, as one sardonic philosopher has observed, that "the person who dies with the most toys wins." Along with these cultural values comes the worldview that supports them. This Western scientific worldview, with its dis-counting of religious values and its emphasis on the material here and now, has had a powerful effect on many of the Buddhist countries' educated classes. In many cases, these groups have rejected Buddhism, equating it with the superstitions of the rural agricul-turalists. This, too, has had an adverse effect on Buddhism.

Should we fear that Buddhism, like so many religions before it, will disappear? Probably not. Such an event is very unlikely. Over the centuries, Buddhism has shown itself to be highly adaptable to new cultural conditions. As we have seen, it spread from its origi-nal home in India throughout most of Asia, coping with new cultures and new languages as it encoun-tered them. In the process, it became an integral part of these cultures. Even now it is changing and adapting. The Buddhism that came to America and Europe from various Asian cultures is being reconceptualized and revitalized in such a manner as to make it uniquely a part of those cultures.

Thailand's Environmental Issues

Buddhism is adapting to the changing environment in its homelands as well. Whereas for many years they were seen as being outside the normal flow of secular society, Buddhist groups whose main focus is on secular social problems are now springing up. A good example of this is currently taking place in Thailand. The Thais are in the process of transforming their economy from an agricultural one to a more industrial model. Unfortunately, as the European experience with the Industrial Revolution showed Westerners, this change is often accompanied by a fearful cost in the quality of human life. Thailand is discovering this for itself.

A particularly severe example of this is the ecological problems the country is now facing. Large tracts of land are being deforested because trees feed the demand for wood products in Japan and elsewhere. This, in turn, results in other problems such as erosion. To combat this, Buddhist groups headed by monks are addressing environmental concerns stemming from the country's rapid industrialization.

Using nonviolent but innovative techniques such as ordaining trees (even Westernized Thais still hold the Sangha in respect and would not cut down an "ordained" tree), these groups are lobbying for the sane use of natural resources based on the Buddhist respect for the integrity of all living beings.

Sri Lanka's Health and Social Issues

In Sri Lanka, monastic organizations are becoming more involved in community health and other social issues in the many tiny villages that dot the island. Traditionally associating with laypersons only to teach and preach, many Buddhist monks are now concerning themselves with more mundane problems. Two good examples of this are Venerable Pandita Walgowwagoda Wimalabuddho Thero of Sri Wardhanaramaya monastery and Venerable Medagama Dhammananda Thero of Asgiri Mahavihara monastery in Kandy.

Pandita Wimalabuddho is a member of the highest council of the Buddhist church in Sri Lanka, but his interests extend beyond purely spiritual matters. One of the programs he has been instrumental in supporting has been a joint program with Japanese Buddhist organizations to combat eye disease in rural areas. These diseases, which cause blindness if left untreated, have always been a problem in the humid tropical climate of the island. Their treatment, which involves the simple application of antibiotic ointment, while relatively cheap, is still beyond the means of the average poor farmer, even if he understands the mechanics of the disease. Through the generosity of Japanese Buddhists, antibiotics are being sent to Sri Lanka and distributed to the villages.

This is not the only example of Buddhist engagement with contemporary problems in Sri Lanka. The

Venerable Dhammananda represents a change that is sweeping through the Buddhist Sangha. A young, well-educated man, Ven Dhammananda was not content to remain in Sri Lanka but traveled to Taiwan to experience Buddhism in that setting. On returning to Sri Lanka, he began to work with laypeople on a variety of social issues. He is emblematic of a change in attitude among younger Buddhist monks as a whole, namely that Buddhism demands engagement with the world, not retreat from it.

On the Right Path

In Sri Lanka, Buddhist laypersons have formed the Sarvodaya Movement to address the socioeconomic problems found in the countryside. This heralds a new day in the relationship of Buddhism to its environment in this ancient society.

Worldwide Social Concerns: AIDS

This reorientation of Buddhism is not happening in traditionally Buddhist countries alone. In the United States, Buddhist teachers and laypersons are a persuasive voice in many areas of social concern. A good example of this is Buddhist work with AIDS sufferers. When the AIDS epidemic initially burst on the American scene, it appeared to be a disease almost exclusively associated with homosexual men. Because homosexual behavior was condemned by traditional Christianity and, therefore, poorly understood by the majority of the American public, AIDS patients were often isolated from traditional spiritual care-givers. Moreover, as the epidemic spread to intra-venous drug users, this stereotypical association of "sin" and AIDS became even more widespread.

Among the first religious groups to oppose this pre-vailing tendency were the American Buddhists. Because Buddhism, by and large, does not maintain the concept of sin and does not condemn homosexu-ality per se, AIDS was not seen as being disgraceful or a just punishment. Rather, it was regarded as just another example of the painful nature of existence, and those suffering from it were seen as fellow beings in need of compassionate treatment. Thus, practicing Buddhists, both gay and straight, were in the forefront of giving care to AIDS patients. Need-less to say, such actions, along with other similar activities such as aiding the homeless, have greatly enhanced the religion's reputation in the United States and Europe.

Women in Western Buddhism

One of the notable features of Buddhism developing in the West is the degree to which women have taken a leading role in transmitting the teachings. Although women have never been excluded from Buddhism, the male-oriented nature of most Asian societies has assigned them a subordinate role in reli-gious matters.

In the West, however, this is not the case. Indeed, many of the pioneers of Buddhist scholarship, such as Mrs. Caroline Rhys-Davids (1858–1942) and I. B. Horner (1896–1981), are still remembered as notable scholars. However, it is as religious teachers that Western women have come into their own.

Bet You Didn't Know

I. B. Horner's book, *Women Under Primitive Buddhism (RAP), Second Edition* (South Asia Books, 1999), provides a perspective on early Indian women's role in Buddhism and monasteries.

One woman who was a particularly interesting example of this was Jiyu Kennett Roshi (Peggy Teresa Nancy Kennett, 1924–1996). British by birth, Kennett Roshi trained first in Western music at London's Trinity College of Music. Increasingly dissatisfied with the life of the Western world, she began to study Buddhism. As one of the first women to receive the approval of Japanese and Korean Zen masters, she was authorized by them to teach.

In 1969, she traveled to the United States and founded Shasta Abbey in Northern California. Since then, her organization, the Order of Buddhist Contemplatives, has founded a number of other monasteries and temples. She wrote a number of books such as *Zen Is Eternal Life*, *How to Grow a Lotus Blossom*, and *Diaries of Years in Japan*.

One might assume that Shasta Abbey would be a faithful recreation of a Japanese monastery, but this is not the case. Kennett Roshi decided early in her career that Buddhism needed to be adapted to the particular conditions of the West. For her, trained as she was in classical Western art and music, this meant taking Western forms and instilling them with a Buddhist spirit.

For example, the Shasta Abbey monks and nuns wear robes that resemble those worn by Christian religious orders. Likewise, the music of the various services is based on Gregorian plainchant, not on Eastern musical models. You might rightly ask if this is the proper way to go about adapting Buddhism to the West, given the fact that these Christian styles no longer resonate with the bulk of the population. Nevertheless, Kennett Roshi's attempts to place Buddhist spirituality within a traditional Western context show the dynamic spirit of American Buddhism and suggest paths for future development.

The Uniqueness of Buddhism

What are the factors that contribute to this continuing appeal of Buddhism and, more particularly, its growing appeal to Europeans and Americans? The simple answer lies in the fact that the problems Buddhism first addressed some 2,500 years ago are still with us today—more or less unchanged.

People still question the nature of life and its ultimate meaning. People still wonder why the good suffer and the evil go unpunished. People still ponder the unstoppable forces of nature and their relationship to human existence. For many of these searchers, the Buddhist analysis of reality and its practical program for achieving transcendence from the pains of human life are very appealing. But other religions, such as Islam, Christianity, and Hinduism, also offer answers to these questions.

Enlighten Me

Buddhism is a means of discovering contentment in the midst of a complicated world, not a way to escape the world's problems or one's own.

Processes vs. Things

One of the features of Buddhism that is attractive to many people, especially people raised in the scientific milieu of Western society, is that Buddhism does away with the idea of the "supernatural," a split between this world and some unseen, totally other reality. The universe, says the Buddhist, is a vast system of processes, not things.

For the Buddhist, one can no more change the inexorable laws of cause and effect than one can hope to repeal the law of gravity. Such a viewpoint is extremely attractive to the Western mind, which has been nurtured on scientific principles. Whereas other religions depend on the unproved (and perhaps unprovable) concept of a supreme deity, Buddhism has no such needs. Moreover, Buddhist presuppositions seem to proceed much more easily from the generally accepted laws of physics, which increasingly seem to support many Buddhist contentions about the nature of the universe, than do theistic presuppositions.

In many ways, Buddhist principles such as cause and effect seem merely to be physical laws applied to the metaphysical realm. Thus, for many people, Buddhism is an increasingly acceptable religious option because it is so "nonreligious," lacking many of the features Westerners deem essential to religion, such as a supreme deity.

Focus on the Individual

Another reason Buddhism maintains its popularity is that it emphasizes individual rather than corporate expressions of religiosity. Among the Western religions, the core religious actions are defined as taking place in community. The believing Christian or Jew is encouraged to attend weekly services in association with his fellow believers. Buddhism, on the other hand, sees religious activity as personal actions. The individual has, of course, opportunities to associate with and take comfort from the community of believers, but he can be just as good a Buddhist without ever encountering another member. It is the internal work of the individual that matters.

In the increasingly individualistic societies of Europe and the United States, this is a distinct advantage, particularly as demands on the individual's time increase and the stately seasonal cycles of ritual that mark Judaism and Christianity become increasingly impractical in a 24/7 industrial world.

Moreover, the individual can practice as much or as little ritualism as he chooses. Whereas the bulk of Western religious activity takes place within the context of formal ritual, Buddhists can practice their religion without any recourse to ritual whatsoever if they choose (although very few people in a traditionally Buddhist country would do so). On the other hand, those who do want to support their meditation practice with more formal rituals can do so easily. Ritual styles are available to suit all tastes in Buddhism, ranging from the relatively austere ritualism of Theravada to the ornate and complex ritualism of Tibetan Buddhism.

Enlighten Me

The Buddha says to be conscious of both good and bad experiences and learn from them. Remember that each thing we do, whether it be large or small, can have an affect on our future, those around us, and even the world.

This appreciation of the personal in Buddhism plays out in other ways as well. Buddhism lacks much of the institutionalized prejudice that exists in other religions. Thus, people of differing races, genders, sexual orientations, and lifestyles find a supportive atmosphere in Buddhism they do not find in Western religions. This is not to say that Buddhism is entirely free of the prejudices that assail other religions—such things as the present troubles in Sri Lanka (see Chapter 9) are ample proof of that. Rather, it is to say that no scriptural or institutional warrant can be the basis for such prejudice, and indeed, much scriptural condemnation of such behavior exists as well. No Buddhist will be able to advance on the spiritual path through the persecution of other religions; quite the contrary, in fact.

Availability

Another appealing Buddhist trait is its long history of using everyday vernacular language rather than a sacred language understood by only a few specialists. The scriptures of the religion are readily available to all its members for study and reflection. This is not to say that the Buddhist scriptures are all of uniform quality or importance, but no privileged ritual language is used in Buddhism.

The scriptures are seen as being just as authoritative in translation as they are in the original languages. In addition, the lack of a mediating priesthood means that each individual Buddhist possesses an equal potential for achieving a realization of ultimate reality without needing to depend on another.

Commitment to Peace

Perhaps the greatest strength of Buddhism is its commitment to peace. In a world that has had two major world wars and innumerable smaller conflicts in the last 100 years, the Buddhist call to peace and human reconciliation is particularly compelling.

There can be little doubt, therefore, that Buddhism will continue to remain a compelling advocate for a gentler world. As long as the problems that mark human existence persist, Buddhism will always find people in every generation for whom its message of hope, peace, and compassion still resonates. It will continue to offer such individuals a way of coping with life's many disappointments and tragedies, and provide an alternate model of human interaction with the world at large. For these people, Buddhism will always be the religion of many paths, but one goal—the goal of peace.

On the Right Path

Buddhist leaders such as the Vietnamese monk Thich Nhat Hanh and the Dalai Lama are regularly nominated for the highest awards as a result of their activities on behalf of peace. These leaders do not preach a message of reconciliation between humans alone. They are also active in crusading on behalf of the mute inhabitants of our planet, demanding that we treat other species and the environment in general with the same respect we want for ourselves. In this, they offer a clear alternative to the prevailing human paradigm of exploitation, both of one another and of the earth.

The Least You Need to Know

- Buddhism is highly adaptable to new cultural conditions, copes with new customs and languages as it encounters them, and even now is changing and adjusting.

- Even though the male-oriented nature of most Asian societies typically assigns women subordinate roles in religious matters, Western Buddhism allows women to take more leading roles in transmitting its teachings.

- Buddhism is an increasingly acceptable religious option because it seems so "nonreligious," meaning it lacks many of the features Westerners deem essential to religion, such as that of a supreme deity.

- It is the internal work of the individual Buddhist that matters; each can practice as much or as little ritualism as he chooses.

- The Buddhist scriptures are just as authoritative in translation as they are in their original languages—and accessible to all.

Glossary

Abhidharma The third of the three divisions of the *Tripitika*, or Buddhist canon. It deals mainly with philosophical problems.

abhiseka A ceremony held mainly in Vajrayana Buddhism to initiate the student into a higher level of study. The number of initiations varies from one tradition to another. *Abhiseka* is literally translated as "sprinkling."

ahimsa The principle, first developed by Jainism, of nonviolence toward other living beings. Practices such as vegetarianism developed from this principle. Ahimsa is now a central tenet of Buddhism.

Amidabutsu The central figure in Pure Land Buddhism. Amidabutsu is the ruler of the "Pure Lands," where it is infinitely easier for Buddhists to achieve nirvana. *Amidabutsu* is literally translated as "the Buddha of Endless Light."

anatman The Buddhist belief that no immortal soul exists, but rather a "cloud" of sensations and processes that human beings mistake for a permanent soul.

anitya The Buddhist belief that everything in the world as we experience it is impermanent.

arhant In Theravada Buddhism, one who has reached nirvana.

asceticism When an individual practices strict self-denial in order to measure his spiritual discipline.

atman   The Hindu idea that an immortal human soul exists that is, in some sense, associated with Brahman.

Bodhisattva   In Mahayana Buddhism, a being who has completed all things necessary to enter nirvana but chooses to postpone his or her own reward in order to help other beings achieve enlightenment as well.

Brahman   In Hinduism, the underlying motivating principle of the universe, the ultimate reality.

Brahmanism   The first phase of Hinduism that was characterized by elaborate sacrificial rituals presided over by the Brahmins.

Brahmins   The highest caste in Hinduism; the priestly class.

caste system   The Hindu idea that society should be divided into hereditary classes.

Confucianism   A belief related to the Chinese philosopher Confucius and his teachings. (Love others; treat others well; follow good morals; and do not try to profit, gain, or take advantage of others.)

Dalai Lama   The head of the Gelugpa school of Tibetan Buddhism. Today the Dalai Lama is the acknowledged spiritual head of Tibetan Buddhism. The present Dalai Lama is the fourteenth of this lineage.

dana   In Theravada Buddhism, the most important lay virtue, which consists of giving material goods liberally to the Buddhist monks.

Dhyana Buddha The Buddhas of universes other than our own. Their name comes from the fact that they are mostly experienced (having communication with) while the disciple is in a meditative state. Dhyana Buddhas are important in the Pure Land tradition.

diorama A miniature, lifelike sculpture displayed such that it blends in with the painting of a realistic background.

dorje A small scepter, usually held in the right hand, that is used in many Tibetan Buddhist rituals. They represent lightning bolts, which in turn represent both skillful means—that is, the practice of using all facets of the human existence to gain enlightenment—and the indestructible, changeless nature of reality (they represent the masculine principle).

duhkha The Buddhist concept that the world is characterized by more unsatisfactory experiences than pleasant ones. *Duhkha* is literally translated as "suffering."

Eightfold Path The Buddha's practical guide, in eight components—right viewpoint, right intention, right speech, right action, right livelihood, right effort, right mindfulness, and right concentration—for escaping the unsatisfactory nature of life.

enlightenment The release from the worldly cycle of birth and death (reincarnation). Enlightenment is the goal of Buddhist practice.

Five Precepts Buddhist ethics that apply to all Buddhists. They consist of refraining from killing, lying, stealing, improper sexual activity, and the taking of intoxicants (drugs and alcohol).

forest monks Monks that continue to hold to the traditional Buddhist monastic ideal of separation from the laity.

Four Noble Truths The basis of Buddhist thought: (1) life is unsatisfactory; (2) it is unsatisfactory because of desire; (3) a way out of the endless series of rebirths exists; (4) that way is the Eightfold Path.

gentry A type of Buddhism that emphasized both Buddhist and Chinese learning and indulged in philosophical discussions and literary activities based on a mixture of Taoist and Buddhist ideas.

ghanta A small hand bell held in the left hand during many Tibetan Buddhist ceremonies (they represent the feminine principle).

guru A teacher, particularly of religion. In Buddhism, a guru is seen as being absolutely essential to spiritual development.

Heart Sutra A central text of Zen Buddhism. The text of the *Heart Sutra* is so short that it can be, and is, chanted in its entirety at most Zen Buddhist ceremonies.

heresy The deviation from a dominant theory or practice.

Jains An early group of Sramanas whose organization and doctrines have many similarities with Buddhism.

Jatakas The stories of the Buddha's previous lives before he became the Buddha. These tales often have a didactic message but also serve as entertainment in Buddhist societies.

karma The idea that actions have inescapable effects, even if those effects are not seen or felt in the present lifetime. Karma is the Indian religions' answer to the problem of evil.

koan A device, usually in the form of a question, used in Zen Buddhist training to force the practitioner to "turn off" the logical, reasoning mind. Very often, no real answer can be made to the questions that koans present.

Lotus Sutra The central scripture of the T'ientai school. The *Lotus Sutra* was begun in India but reached its most profound development in China.

Lotus position The cross-legged position most commonly used for meditation practice.

Mahayana A school of Buddhism that predominates in China, Korea, Vietnam, and Japan. Mahayana is literally translated as "the Great Vehicle."

mandala A sacred drawing or design that provides the practitioner with a sort of "road map" of reality. Mandalas are very frequently used in Tibetan Buddhist practices.

mantra A sacred formula used in some forms of Buddhist meditation. Although common to all forms of Buddhism, mantras are particularly utilized in Tibetan practice.

mindfulness The foundation for all Buddhist spiritual practice. Mindfulness is the idea that a person must "wake up" and live life consciously and deliberately.

mudra Gesture made with the hands. Mudras are particularly important in Tibetan Buddhist rituals as the union of the *dorjes* and *ghantas* (the masculine and feminine principles) is an enlightened mind.

nirvana The goal of Buddhist practice. It is the opposite of *samsara*, the world we inhabit right now. Other than it being different in every way from anything experienced in this world, the Buddhists are hesitant to try to describe nirvana.

pabbajja To leave the world, begin ordination as a novice, and adopt the ascetic life.

Pali A dialect of Sanskrit, Pali is the language of the oldest collection of Buddhist scriptures and the sacred language of Theravada Buddhism.

Parinirvana The indescribable ultimate when an individual has attained complete detachment from all physical and emotional suffering caused by a state of unhappiness. It is also detachment from the states of satisfaction, happiness, and nirvana (escaping the cycle of samsara, or reincarnation). Parinirvana is the final nirvana—perfect tranquility.

phurba   A ritual dagger used to cut off "ignorance" in Tibetan Buddhist rituals.

poya days   The "Sundays" or Sabbath days of Theravada Buddhism. They happen twice each lunar month on the days of the full and new moons. On these days, pious Buddhists perform a variety of religious activities, including giving food to the monks, listening to sermons, and strictly adhering to the Five Precepts.

pratitya-samutpada   The Buddhist concept that the world is made up of an endless series of interlocking events (preexisting conditions).

puja   In Hinduism and Buddhism, a ceremony designed to honor divine figures.

punya   The idea that good actions produce merit. This merit, in Theravada Buddhism at least, can be "traded" to the gods in return for material favors.

Pure Land Sutras   The collection of texts that describe the Pure Land. The *Pure Land Sutras* are the scriptural foundation of the various Pure Land Schools.

reincarnation   The idea, common to all Indic religions, that human beings are "recycled" lifetime after lifetime. Far from being a good thing, reincarnation is seen as something to escape from at all costs, by becoming enlightened and ending the cycle of birth and rebirth.

Rig Vega   The oldest of the Hindu scriptures.

Rinzai   One of the two predominant schools of Zen Buddhism. The Rinzai school makes extensive use of *koans* in its training. *See also* Soto.

samadhi   The lower of the two stages of Buddhist meditation (*vipasyana* being the higher). Samadhi consists primarily of quieting the mind.

samsara   The opposite of nirvana, samsara is the world as we experience it and is something to be escaped from by attaining enlightenment.

Sangha   Strictly speaking, sangha is all Buddhists. In practice, the term tends to refer only to ordained Buddhist monks and nuns.

Sanskrit   The sacred language of Hinduism and India in general. Although it is a dead language today, it is distantly related to English, Spanish, and French.

schism   A formal division in or separation from religious tenets based on conflicting beliefs.

Shingon   A religion that was established by Kôbô Daishi (Kûkai) at the beginning of the Heian period (ninth century); the teachings are known as Shingon Esoteric Buddhism.

skillful means   A term common to all forms of Buddhism but predominant in Mahayana Buddhism, it is used to describe the idea that an advanced Buddhist sage can use actions that appear wrong or immoral in order to lead disciples to the greater good of a religious life.

sky burial   A Tibetan Buddhist ritual in which the deceased is cut into pieces and left to be devoured by predatory birds. This is done to bring the deceased good karma in his next life.

Soto   The second of the great schools of Zen. Unlike *Rinzai*, Soto Zen tends to eliminate use of the *koan* and concentrates on "just sitting." *See also* Rinzai.

Sramanas   A religious movement that broke away from the prevailing Brahmanic school of Hinduism. It is from the Sramanas that both Buddhism and Jainism developed.

stupa   A building or a large mound of earth raised over relics of the Buddha. Stupas are popular places for Buddhist pilgrimages.

sunyata   The Mahayana concept that ultimately nothing has any independent reality or enduring substance in itself.

Sutras   The second of the divisions of the Buddhist cannon *Tripitika*, the Sutras contain the sermons and stories of the Buddha.

Tantra   A form of religious practice common to both Buddhism and Hinduism that places major emphasis on elaborate rituals performed by the individual practitioner.

Taoism   A Chinese mystical philosophy that teaches conformity to the Tao through modest actions and minimalism (a simplistic life).

Theravada The oldest form of institutional Buddhism, this school places emphasis on meditation and a disciplined way of life. Theravada is the predominant form of Buddhism in Sri Lanka, Burma (Myanmar), Thailand, Laos, and Cambodia. Theravada is literally translated as "the Way of the Elders."

Three Marks of Existence The fundamental philosophical basis of Buddhism that says (1) the material world is constantly changing, (2) human life is ultimately unsatisfying, and (3) no permanent human soul exists that moves from one life to another.

Three Refuges The act of publicly declaring one's allegiance to the Buddha, his teachings, and the Buddhist Order.

Tripitika The Buddhist canon, divided into the Vinaya, the Sutras, and the Abhidharma.

trsna The Buddhist idea that all unhappiness comes from desire (literally "thirst") or greed for possessions.

tulku The reborn head of a monastic lineage in Tibet. The tulku best known in the West is the Dalai Lama.

twilight language In Vajrayana Buddhism, twilight language is a deliberately obscure way of writing designed to protect its teachings from unauthorized practitioners. Twilight language can only be interpreted through the guidance of a guru or teacher.

Upanishads A series of philosophical writings first collected near the end of the Vedic Period (c. 800 to 400 B.C.E.). A number of ideas found in the *Upanishads* have parallels in Buddhist and Jain literature.

upasampada The rite of entrance into the Buddhist monkhood. It is considered the highest ordination.

Vajrayana The third and latest of the major divisions of Buddhism, this school places a great deal of emphasis on ritualism. Once much more widespread than at present, Vajrayana is currently practiced mostly in Tibet.

village monks Monks that live on the periphery of a village and act as schoolteachers and local religious advisors to the laity. These monks minister to everyday people.

Vinaya The first of the divisions of the *Tripitika*, this deals with the rules governing monks and nuns in Buddhism.

Vipasyana The second and higher level of Buddhist meditation designed to lead the practitioner to enlightenment (*samadhi* being the lower level). Vipasyana consists primarily of analytical and insightful meditation.

yidam In Tibetan Buddhism, a yidam is a personal deity who plays a central part in the practitioner's meditative and ritual life.

yoga A series of practical exercises designed to allow the practitioner to penetrate the nature of reality. Yoga is used in both Hinduism and Buddhism.

Zen A school of Mahayana Buddhism that places its emphasis on meditative exercises rather than scriptural study. Found predominantly in China, Korea, and Japan, Zen has also been very influential in America and Europe in recent decades.

Index